WHAT PEOPLE AR

ROMEO AND JULI

A book of vivid first-hand experience about the daily lives, suffering and courage of Palestinians living in the West Bank. Read it, imagine it and pass it around.

**John Berger**

Cool and understated, *Romeo and Juliet in Palestine* is at once a finely observant account of a teacher at work in the Occupied Territories and a cumulatively powerful indictment of the systematic constraints young Palestinian men and women experience, as they try to get a university education in difficult times. Sperlinger comes across as a gifted, sympathetic, and resourceful classroom teacher, wonderfully inventive in his approach to his texts and to his students, humorous, hard on himself, open to all the strangeness of his situation. This is a wise and moving document.

**Neil Hertz**, author of *Pastoral in Palestine* and Professor Emeritus at Johns Hopkins University

It's often said that *Romeo and Juliet* is a universal tale, carrying its story of love across languages and cultures. Tom Sperlinger's elegantly-written prose instead gently unpicks the array of meanings, experiences and emotions which his Palestinian university students find in Shakespeare. Reminiscent of Azar Nafisi's *Reading Lolita in Tehran*, this is a wise, humble meditation on knowledge, learning, and the challenges of imagining a life beyond occupation.

**Sarah Irving**, author of *Leila Khaled: Icon of Palestinian Liberation* and *The Bradt Guide to Palestine* and co-editor of *A Bird is Not a Stone: An Anthology of Contemporary Palestinian Poetry*

This honest and thoughtful memoir is also a good introduction to a slice of Palestinian reality. Sperlinger has the decency not to pretend to understand everything he sees; the reader learns along with him. When he and his students at Abu Dis achieve a moment of connection over English literature (even as Sperlinger struggles with the postcolonial implications of what he is doing) the reader is moved.

**Margaret Litvin**, author of *Hamlet's Arab Journey: Shakespeare's Prince and Nasser's Ghost*

*Romeo and Juliet in Palestine* has a visionary force and clarity.
**Tom Paulin**

# Romeo and Juliet in Palestine

## Teaching Under Occupation

# Romeo and Juliet in Palestine

## Teaching Under Occupation

Tom Sperlinger

Winchester, UK
Washington, USA

First published by Zero Books, 2015
Zero Books is an imprint of John Hunt Publishing Ltd., Laurel House, Station Approach,
Alresford, Hants, SO24 9JH, UK
office1@jhpbooks.net
www.johnhuntpublishing.com
www.zero-books.net

For distributor details and how to order please visit the 'Ordering' section on our website.

Text copyright: Tom Sperlinger 2014

ISBN: 978 1 78279 637 4
Library of Congress Control Number: 2014957342

Design: Lee Nash

Printed and bound by CPI Group (UK) Ltd, Croydon, CR0 4YY, UK

We operate a distinctive and ethical publishing philosophy in all
areas of our business, from our global network of authors to
production and worldwide distribution.

# CONTENTS

*We are always educating for a world that is or is becoming out of joint.*
Hannah Arendt


*It is a well-known fact that Shakespeare is a Palestinian.*
Amir Nizar Zuabi

Romeo and Juliet in Palestine

الى طلابي

ix

# Author's note

This book is an account of the spring semester in 2013, during which I taught English Literature at Al-Quds University in Abu Dis, in the occupied West Bank. It includes stories that my students told me as well as some of the experiences that we shared in class. I have changed some names and various details to protect the identities of those involved.

During the semester, I taught two classes, Shakespearean Drama and Special Topics in Literature. I refer throughout the book to several of the key texts we used. All quotations from *Romeo and Juliet* are from the 2012 Arden edition edited by René Weis; references to *Julius Caesar* are from the 2004 updated edition of the New Cambridge Shakespeare edited by Marvin Spevack.

Romeo and Juliet in Palestine

# 1

# Romeo and Juliet in Palestine

Just before 2pm, on a warm day in March, three students came into the office and told me that campus was being evacuated.

I had finished teaching just after noon and walked up towards the English Department office. Al-Quds University is on a hillside, levelled into a series of plateaus connected by steep concrete steps. When I reached the top, I heard a shout and I caught a glimpse of movement in the square below. Recently students had gathered there to support Samer Issawi and other Palestinian prisoners on hunger strike in Israeli gaol. At first, I thought it was another protest. But a gang of twenty or thirty boys was marching across the square. They were mostly teenagers, although some looked younger. They were shouting and brandishing bats, sticks, and strips of wood torn from fences, as they marched up the steps in front of me.

'Don't be scared,' someone whispered. I was standing with a few other teachers. 'You should go inside,' a woman who sounded American told me: 'You have an English accent.' I discovered later that students at nearby Birzeit University had confronted a British diplomat a few days before.

When I heard that campus was being evacuated, I was waiting to meet students who were due to take an exam. I found a colleague, Ahmed, who also lived in Ramallah, and we left together. Security guards had closed off the glass doors at the end of the building, which we would normally have used. A fight was taking place on the road outside. We made our way back down the steps, at the bottom of which there was now a Red Crescent ambulance. 'The problem is that people think they will be martyrs if they die,' said Ahmed, who told me that he had heard gunshots while he was teaching. Later, he said that some boys fought to impress girls.

Outside campus, people were streaming in every direction, trying to leave. Ahmed and I eventually got into a *servees*, one of the minibuses that are used as shared taxis. I was wedged in behind the gap between the two front seats. It could take up to an hour to get back to Ramallah, and sometimes the *servees* went terrifyingly fast. But it was an unusually quiet journey home.

On the morning of the fight, we had finished reading *Romeo and Juliet*. The Shakespeare course I was teaching was a slow pleasure. At home, on a module of this kind, we might read nine or ten plays, skating the surface at a rate of one a week. Here we spent several weeks reading each play aloud, almost line by line. The closing scene of *Romeo and Juliet* worked well as a finale, partly because it requires so many voices. There were 40 students in the class.

I asked the students how the play might be adapted as a film in Palestine. One young woman said she would set the film in the present because the Palestinians are at the peak of their troubles, economically and politically. Another said she would set it in the late 1940s or 50s, when there had been a famous dispute between two families in Jerusalem. A third said the play could be set at any time in Palestine because of the violent context. Most of the students thought that Verona ought to be Jerusalem and that Romeo might be banished to Ramallah or Gaza, or somewhere in Jordan, in place of Mantua. One suggestion was that Juliet might be from Jerusalem and Romeo from the West Bank: their difficulties would then arise from the fact that they have different ID cards. The Oslo Accords of 1993 divided Palestinians into different 'groups' with separate forms of ID for the West Bank, Gaza and Jerusalem. My students wrestled with similar practical difficulties. One told me he was engaged but didn't know when he could marry because he had a West Bank card and his fiancée had a Jerusalem one. Other ideas were that Juliet should be a Christian Palestinian and Romeo a

Muslim, or Romeo could be Israeli and Juliet could be a Palestinian. ('That happens a lot,' one young woman said.) Another student said that if it were an Israeli/Palestinian conflict, the ending would have to change, because the Montagues and Capulets would never join hands.

I wondered what the students would cut or add in a film version of the play. 'I'd cut the kiss,' said one woman, 'because of their age.' 'More kissing!' retorted several men. 'Cut Rosaline,' another woman said with a sigh. (She'd earlier lamented how fickle Romeo could be.) 'Make them older,' someone said. 'Cut the Nurse!' 'Cut all of the long speeches!' 'Put in a song.' One student said the play should be in modern slang, with the Nurse speaking in dialect. A man said he would draw out the action over a month, rather than five days, to make the love story more plausible. 'Give it a happy ending!' But if Romeo and Juliet live, I suggested, the Montagues and Capulets can't be reconciled. So would they want Romeo and Juliet to escape together into exile? 'Yes!' a few roared. 'To Gaza?' I asked, to general laughter. 'To Jordan,' they suggested.

The students continued to re-imagine the play in a piece of homework. In a rewrite by a student called Qais, Romeo was Rami, a resident of Ramallah, and Juliet was Juweida, from Barta'a, a Palestinian village in Israel. Qais set the play towards the end of the second intifada, the Palestinian uprising in 2000-2005, during which it was nearly impossible for young men like Rami to go into Israel. Rami and Juweida can only meet on the internet, and 'as if the existing political issues aren't enough, their main problem is surprisingly family tradition'. Both families are Arab and both feel 'bitterness' about the Palestinians' plight. But Juweida's family are Israeli citizens and think 'they are privileged and live within a modern, stable "country" and view Rami as a broke loser.'

Qais re-wrote the scene in which Romeo hears of Juliet's apparent death. In his version, Rami is visited by his friend,

3

Ameen, who tells him that Juweida has transferred her affections to a rich Israeli Arab, the term applied to Palestinians who are citizens of Israel. Qais noted that 'for a big minority of Palestinian youth, using English as one third of their daily speech is normal' and that the lovers are 'fans of foreign dialects of English and are particularly obsessed with a rapper from Liverpool.' And so he used a mix of Shakespearean verse, Arabic and Scouse for the encounter between Rami and Ameen:

> *Ameen*: Allo, my kidda.
> *Rami*: *Marhaba* Ameen, what hath made you such a beanie this morning? Is my Judy well?
> *Ameen*: She is well, better than thee and I!
> Let it bother you not, she may have been a sloobag...
> *Rami*: Ya *kalb*! Mark your words, for you be speaking of my beloved!
> *Ameen*: I would've ne'er spoken ill of someone I've not seen doing ill. Your Ju was with a smile next to a soft lad with a Merc...

I had lived in Liverpool for several years and was surprised to see familiar Scouse terms—'kidda' (young guy), 'judy' (young woman), 'beanie' (annoying person), 'sloobag' (promiscuous person), and 'soft lad' (idiot)—alongside Arabic words I was learning, such as '*marhaba*' for 'hello' and '*kalb*' for 'dog'.

Another student, Woroud, set her version of the play during the Six Day War in 1967. In her version, Romeo is Saleem and Juliet is Jamila and there are 'no fights or disputes between the two families'. Instead, they are separated by the events of the war. In the scene that Woroud re-wrote, the two families are hiding in a deserted cave in Jericho, having walked long distances to escape 'Israeli bombs and explosions' and to protect 'their daughters and kids from rapes and kidnappings'. Saleem and Jamila must part from one another—as the lovers part after their only night together in the play—because Saleem's family is leaving for Lebanon.

> *Saleem*: *Habibtie*, by the blessed moon up there
> That tips with silver all these fruit-tree tops, I swear
> to look for you the seven earths.
> *Jamila*: O, don't swear by the moon, the inconstant moon,
> That monthly goes through changes in her circled orbit,
> For fear that your love prove as variable as the moon.
> *Saleem*: What shall I swear by?
> *Jamila*: (crying) Don't swear at all
> Or if you will, swear by Allah,
> Which is the god that we worship,
> the god who sees us right now
> And I'll believe you.
> *Saleem*: I swear by Allah; *Al Qadeer*.
> *Jamila*: Although I have joy in you,
> I'm very sad this night;
> Look at this bud of love that, ripened by summer's breezes,
> May become a beautiful flower when next we meet.
> *Saleem*: Insha'Allah
> *Jamila*: Insha'Allah

Woroud's version was not the only one to offer glimpses inside Palestinian history. Other students set the play during the first intifada in the late 1980s, in present-day Gaza, or in 1948, when Israel was founded and many Palestinians were expelled from their land.

In our first class on the play, I'd asked the students: why is it dangerous for Romeo and Juliet to fall in love? 'Because their parents hate each other,' they replied. 'Why?' I asked. The lack of an explanation for this hatred may be one reason the play is so effective. It is typical of the gaps in Shakespeare's plays, which leave them open to interpretation. However, there is also an absence of authority in the play. As Hannah Arendt has written: 'Violence appears where power is in jeopardy.' In one discussion, the students probed the relationship between the Prince and the two families. Why does he struggle to be heard by the families, or to impose his will on them? Is he, as in the Baz Luhrmann film version, something closer to a chief of police and thus an agent of the law rather than a man in power?

Over the weeks that followed I picked up anecdotal scraps of information, sometimes contradictory, about what had happened that day on campus. The boys who had arrived were from Sawahera, a village next to Abu Dis, which is divided in two by the Wall. Apparently they'd been pursuing a dispute with a boy from Abu Dis, who was studying at the university. I was told it was about a girl, but also that it was part of a series of skirmishes between two families. Nobody seemed sure about the origins of the feud, which had been going on for several years.

The West Bank is carved into three administrative areas, with 60% in Area C, under full Israeli control. Area A, which makes up 18%, is under Palestinian Authority civil and security control. It includes Ramallah, and other cities in the West Bank, and Israeli citizens are forbidden from entering these areas (although during military crackdowns the Israeli Defence Force has invaded them). The Abu Dis campus is situated in Area B, which is under Palestinian civil control and joint Israeli-Palestinian security control, but which is effectively lawless. There is often tension in Abu Dis between Israeli forces and the local population. On several occasions, our classes were disrupted by tear gas, fired by Israeli soldiers at local teenagers. Amira Hass wrote in the Israeli newspaper *Ha'aretz* in 2011: 'Palestinian police are unable to operate in the area around Abu Dis, but Israeli forces don't appear interested in stopping the villages from becoming a breeding ground for drug dealers and crime.' As a consequence of this power vacuum, she noted, a 'conflict between two families' in the area can spin 'out of control'.

Whenever 'trouble' erupted in the West Bank while I was there—when there was a modest rise in the tension, for example after a Palestinian prisoner died in an Israeli gaol—the most visible sign was young boys and teenagers on the streets, armed with stones and catapults. On the way home from campus one evening, in a *servees*, we passed a boy of about ten who was standing at the centre of a mini-roundabout, hurling stones. As we turned right off the roundabout, in the direction he had thrown them, we passed a burning tyre. A hundred yards behind it were a couple of Israeli soldiers. As we moved parallel with them, one of the soldiers tossed a stone up in the air and caught it. Hillel Frisch, an expert on the conflict from Bar-Ilan University, told *The Guardian* in February 2013: 'The people being wounded in [the current] clashes are 13 and 16-year-old kids, not the 17 to 32-year-old men [who] have been either decimated or incarcerated since the second intifada.' In the same week as the fight on campus, UNICEF released a report on the treatment of children in Israeli military detention. It stated that children aged 12-13 years old can be imprisoned for up to 6 months for throwing stones, or 5 years if they are 14-15, and those over 16 for ten years. The report concluded: 'Ill-treatment of Palestinian children in the Israeli military detention system appears to be widespread, systematic and institutionalized.'

For a couple of days after the fight, the university was closed. I kept in touch with my students by e-mail and through a Facebook group they had started. There were lots of rumours about the fight. One student, called Haytham, wrote to me to explain that there had been another fight of a similar kind a few months before:

> The guy who died [in the earlier fight] was my friend, and he's from the same village [as me]. The guys who did this were his cousins, and best friends. They wanted to take revenge of him but never kill him but it went bad and the

knife managed to work deeper than expected. He was killed in front of my eyes. The ones who killed him are in jail now and one of them is crying till this moment as he never wanted to kill his cousin. He was one hell of a good friend and we all got shocked of the fact of his death but yet we're kinda used and always ready to lose close friends.

* * *

In this book, I try to tell the story of the semester I spent at Al-Quds. It is a story about the particular students and colleagues I encountered and is not intended as a general account of life in Palestine or at the university. I rely on anecdotes drawn from memory or adapted from a diary I kept while I was living in the West Bank. I said to a student during the semester that the worst kind of class is one in which the teacher knows how the discussion will end. I suspect the same is true for a book, and I hope that the reader can interpret these anecdotes in his or her own way.

However, any book about Israel and Palestine involves engaging with a complex political reality, so I will begin by saying something about the experiences and perspectives that inform this account. My father, David, was born in London in 1948, the same year that the state of Israel was founded. His parents, Tibor and Lisl Sperlinger, had fled Vienna in 1938. They were Jewish and throughout their adult lives they were committed Zionists. I will occasionally draw on an interview which my father recorded with Lisl in the late 1990s, in which she talked about her life.

Zionism emerged as a political force in the late nineteenth century. There were suggestions early on that a state in Palestine might be shared between Jews and other faiths, or that a Jewish homeland might be created elsewhere. In the early 1900s, the British Government had explored whether the Zionists could be offered a portion of British East Africa, an idea called 'The Uganda Scheme'. In 1917, the Balfour Declaration, written by the-then Foreign Secretary, committed the British Government to 'view with favour the establishment of a national home for the Jewish people' in Palestine, which was then under British rule. Balfour noted equivocally that 'nothing shall be done which may prejudice the civil and religious rights of existing non-Jewish communities'.

The urgency of the Zionist cause quickened in the 1930s and 1940s. Israel's narratives about itself are inextricably linked with the Holocaust, as are the stories of those people, like my grand-parents, who supported the cause for a Jewish homeland while being persecuted by the Nazis. In May 1942, when Zionist leaders met at the Biltmore Hotel in New York, they wanted to offer 'a message of hope and encouragement to their fellow Jews in the Ghettos and concentration-camps.' The conference was the first time that the Zionist movement clearly defined its aim 'that Palestine be established as a Jewish commonwealth.' In 1944, the American Zionist Organisation went further, calling for a commonwealth that would 'embrace the whole of Palestine, undivided and undiminished.' Hannah Arendt, the German-Jewish thinker who had fled to the States, wrote that this was 'a turning point in Zionist history': '[It] goes even a step further than the Biltmore Programme, in which the Jewish minority had granted minority rights to the Arab majority. This time the Arabs were simply not mentioned in the resolution, which obviously leaves them the choice between voluntary emigration or second-class citizenship.'_

Haytham was 23 in 2013. He and the other students I taught at Al-Quds were born under occupation. When they were still toddlers, the Oslo Accords, which were seen in the West as a hopeful development, divided the West Bank into three different areas (A, B, and C), dramatically restricting the movement of Palestinians within the occupied territories, including their right to live where they chose. For this reason, some have compared Oslo to the founding of apartheid in South Africa rather than its conclusion. The West Bank lies to the east of Israel, with Gaza to its west. These two strips of land were occupied by Israel in 1967, during the war that Woroud dramatised in her version of *Romeo and Juliet*. The occupation was not only all that my students had known; it had been the backdrop to their parents' whole lives as well. If you live in an occupied land, you do not have many of the rights associated with being a citizen, including the right to property, a fair trial, or to travel unhindered. This is the context in which children in the West Bank can be imprisoned for, among other things, throwing stones.

Since 1967, divisions have been created between groups of Palestinians, a process that was embedded after Oslo. On a small scale, I could pick up tensions between those students with a West Bank ID card and those with a Jerusalem ID, since the latter had more freedom of movement and a slightly wider range of opportunities after graduating. These different IDs were introduced in the late 1960s, but since the 1990s the cards have been issued by the Palestinian Authority (PA). The PA was established in 1994, as a step towards creating the government for a Palestinian state. While I was in the West Bank, disillusionment with the PA ran very deep. Many openly compared it to administrations in former British and French colonies, in which local people were enlisted to enforce imperial rule. In Gaza, similar frustrations led to Hamas, a Palestinian Islamic organisation, winning a majority in parliamentary elections in 2006. Hamas was a visible presence in the West Bank too, although the more moderate faction of Fatah was dominant.

The split between the two factions is, in part, a division between generations. Sari Nusseibeh, a philosopher and former Fatah politician who was president of Al-Quds while I was there, was born in 1949. He too was born without a country, at a time when Jerusalem and the West Bank were part of Jordan. Sari came to prominence in the first intifada, which lasted from 1987 to the early 1990s, and which was characterised by a mass civil disobedience movement. He wrote the Fourteen Demands, which were published in January 1988. The first Demand was that Israel should abide by the 1949 Fourth Geneva Convention, which was established to protect civilians during wartime, following the Nazi atrocities. It includes specific provision for the treatment of those living under an occupying power, preventing collective punishment and individual or mass forced transfers.

When they were teenagers, my students' lives had been overshadowed by the second intifada (the Arabic word means 'shaking off'), which was the setting for Qais's re-writing of Shakespeare's play. The uprising began in 2000 and included several years of extraordinary violence. There was a series of suicide bombings by Palestinians in Israel and the military regime in the West Bank and Gaza became increasingly brutal. My students recalled that their schools were closed for long periods. When I was in the West Bank, there was ongoing specu-lation that a third intifada might erupt. But the Palestinian political leadership was divided and many young men had been imprisoned or killed, so it was not clear who would lead any mass resistance.

If you listen to the news in the UK, you will probably hear about Israel/Palestine as an intractable conflict and it may sound as though it is between two equal sides, each with a claim to the same land. The only possible solution you will hear discussed is for there to be two states. During my time in the West Bank, I didn't hear anyone claim that two states was a plausible way forward. The West Bank is a relatively small strip of land (about a quarter of the size of Wales), with little strategic capacity to defend itself, and it now has around 515,000 Israeli settlers living in it, according to the Israeli human rights organisation B'Tselem. This includes East Jerusalem, which is recognised as occupied under international law, but which is on the Israeli side of the Wall. Many of the Palestinians I spoke to were in favour of one democratic state in the whole of Israel/Palestine, for all of the people who live there. They saw this as the only possible solution, in an area where the Christian, Jewish and Muslim populations are intertwined and where until recently they lived in relatively peaceful co-existence. The case for one state has been made by Sari Nusseibeh in *What is a Palestinian State Worth?*, as well as by the journalist Ali Abunimah in *One Country* and the Israeli activist Jeff Halper in *An Israeli in Palestine*.

The two-state solution resembles in some respects the proposal made by the United Nations in 1947 for the partition of Palestine. The Israeli and Palestinian accounts of what happened in 1948 have always diverged. The Zionist movement accepted the proposal but the Muslim and Christian populations did not. A war ensued, and the Israeli state was established in an area of land larger than the UN had agreed. In Israel, the events of 1948 are celebrated as a struggle for independence. For Palestinians, what happened in 1948 is referred to as the '*nakba*' or the 'catastrophe'. When the United Nations Relief and Works Agency (UNRWA) was founded in 1951, to deal with the Palestinian refugee crisis, there were about 750,000 refugees. Today, more than five million people, scattered across different continents, are registered as eligible for UNRWA's services. They have not been offered the right to return to their land or compensation for their loss.

In 2006, the Israeli historian Ilan Pappe produced a contro-versial account of 1948, which was closer to the Palestinian narrative. He argued that there was a planned and forced expulsion of the Arab and Christian populations by Zionist forces:

When it was over, more than half of Palestine's native population, close to 800,000 people, had been uprooted, 531 villages had been destroyed, and eleven urban neighbour-hoods emptied of their inhabitants. The [Zionist] plan decided upon on 10 March 1948, and above all its systematic implementation in the following months, was a clear-cut case of an ethnic cleansing operation, regarded under international law today as a crime against humanity.

## 2

# No such place

'Are you Jewish?'

'My father's Jewish.'

'And your mother?'

As we spoke, he turned slightly away, writing with his left hand on a clipboard. When he had finished writing, his hand would twitch up automatically to adjust his glasses.

'She's Christian,' I replied.

'Where is she from?'

'Belfast.'

'Why did your father marry her?'

I didn't think this was a question I could answer.

'Do you know any Hebrew?'

'I learnt a little at university.'

He asked me a question I did not understand.

'I didn't learn that much.'

'Do you want to take it up again?'

'Maybe.'

'Who will you be visiting in Israel?'

I gave the names of my relatives and, in a routine I remembered from family holidays, I tried to work out how I was related to my grandmother's first cousin and his descendants.

He interrupted me: 'Have you met them before?'

'Yes, in London.'

'When were you last in Israel?'

'This is my first visit.'

Until now, the security guard had looked at me with a practiced intensity. Now he grinned, and his arms opened.

'You're so lucky!'

On the morning of my first visit to Al-Quds University, in 2011, I couldn't find it on a map. I was due to give a paper in the English Department. I established that I would be visiting the campus in the West Bank, but my guidebook made only passing mention of Abu Dis. I was staying in Jerusalem and I picked up a taxi just outside the Old City. We took a looping route through villages and side roads, to avoid any checkpoints, before eventually circling the university about forty minutes later. For a minute or two, just before campus, the road curved and the Wall seemed to cling to it, so that it was all I could see on the horizon.

I was met by Jalal, a graduate of the university in his 20s, who spoke with a hint of a Sheffield accent. He had spent a year studying in England. The campus was decorated with dozens of flags for Fatah, Hamas and other student factions. Jalal explained that they were in the run-up to a student election. There was a rally in progress, and before I could see it, I heard it: a young man's voice was booming out over a microphone.

I was given a tour of the university's Abu Jihad museum. The building is designed to resemble a prison. You enter through a metal revolving door; there is also a representation of the Wall outside, to symbolise that the West Bank and Gaza are also prisons. The displays included artworks and posters about the prisoners' movement, letters, information on international law, and an exhibition about the experiences of women, children and families affected by the prison experience. Salam Fayyad, who was then Prime Minister of the PA, stated in 2012 that 800,000 Palestinians had been imprisoned since 1967, which is about 20% of the total population and 40% of the male population. Jalal pulled me aside, to show me his favourite poster. It was a white canvas, with the silhouette of an empty glass bottle running vertically down the left-hand side. Nestled in the bottom of the bottle was a man, sitting in a crouched position with his arms locked around his knees. The man's face was in shadow. The caption read: 'Thirst for freedom'. An academic I met later that day told me that the museum had been consciously modelled on how the Holocaust is memorialised.

I had sent the university a list of possible topics I could give a paper on. When it was time, I was placed at the end of a long table, with about thirty staff and students crowded into the room. The academic who was to introduce me explained to me quietly, before we started, that he was not a literature professor. He said a few words, cribbed from my university webpage at home, and concluded: 'I am sure this will be a very interesting talk. I don't know anything about George Eliot, but I do know she was a Zionist.'

Ahmed wanted to talk to me about my paper before he took me to sit in on his class. He explained that he had read some of Eliot's works while writing his PhD thesis on D.H. Lawrence, at a university in India. Ahmed was in his late 30s. He was tall and neatly dressed. Later, a colleague would describe him as thick-skinned, because students playing up rarely fazed him. Even when I saw Ahmed moved to anger, it still seemed encased inside this attitude of restraint, as if it did not come naturally to him. He spoke in a measured and precise English. I asked him how he had got interested in Lawrence. '*Sons and Lovers*,' he said crisply, through cigarette smoke.

There were about thirty students in Ahmed's American Literature class. They were sitting in rows, and each chair had a flat wooden table attached to its armrest. The young men in the class were mostly dressed in jeans and loose-fitting sweatshirts. The women were divided between a small number, also in jeans and with their hair hanging down over their shoulders, and the majority whom wore dresses, long cardigans or a loose robe with long sleeves, and most of who wore the hijab. Ahmed had to work to keep the students' attention, and there were bursts of chattering and whispered asides. They had been reading Thoreau's 'Civil Disobedience':

Under a government which imprisons any unjustly, the true place for a just man is also a prison [...] Thus the State never intentionally confronts a man's sense, intellectual or moral, but only his body, his senses. It is not armed with superior wit or honesty, but with superior physical strength.

Ahmed guided the students through the passage, clarifying some of the language and prompting them about the argument. I could not tell whether the students were following. I was sitting to the side, by the window, and Ahmed had left a pile of marking on the table in front of me, ready to return to the students. I glanced through the paper on the top. The handwriting was small and neat, but the sentences seemed disconnected and the sheet was decorated with red circles and corrections.

About ten minutes before the end of class, Ahmed turned to me: 'Now our visitor will address you,' he said. On an impulse, I asked the students to tell me why they were at university. There was a short silence. A young man spoke and told me that his name was Tariq. He was leaning back in his chair, so that its front legs tilted slightly off the ground. He said, with a slight smile: 'It's all a waste of time.'

I knew this was a challenge and I weighed my answer carefully so that it did not seem dismissive. 'So why are you wasting your time *here*?'

One woman said that she was at university because she liked studying; a male student said, more equivocally, that he was there because of his parents. One of the women said she wanted to learn English so as to get a good job, and there were a few murmurs of assent. 'There are no jobs,' Tariq countered.

The next class was on Shakespeare's sonnets. Ahmed spent the first half of it sketching out a brief history of the sonnet form, explaining how Shakespeare had transformed it from its Italian origins. This time when he asked me to speak at the end, I felt better prepared. 'I want you to imagine that I am a musician,' I

17

said. 'I'm visiting from England, and I have brought this new kind of song with me, which everyone in England is playing. You're a group of musicians too. But you haven't heard of this song, and when I play it, you want to start making your own version in Arabic. How would the song change?'

The students told me a little about how Arabic and English were different and how the song might change to accommodate new rhymes, but also to reflect different experiences. Ahmed chipped in, to explain that when sonnet 18 is translated into Arabic it is altered, from 'Shall I compare thee to a summer's day?' to 'Shall I compare thee to a spring day?' In the Middle East, spring is the more pleasant season, he said, so that to ask 'Shall I compare thee to a summer's day?' would be almost an insult ('You make me sweaty and uncomfortable'). We were running out of time. I asked one more question, which I said the students should think about before their next class: 'Shakespeare was a very successful playwright by the time he started writing sonnets. Why did he start to write poems instead?' We touched briefly on the fact that the playhouses were closed because of plague in the 1590s, and that this may have been one reason why Shakespeare turned to a different form.

As Ahmed and I were leaving, Tariq chased after us in the corridor. He had been sitting at the back of the Shakespeare class, but he had not spoken. I was slightly unnerved, as he dashed towards us, and his face gave nothing away. He was gesturing at the textbook he was holding. 'Do you think Shakespeare wanted to say something personal, which he could not say in a play?' he asked me. 'Was *he* in love?'

Ahmed left me in one of the department offices, while he went off to a meeting. The room was full of cigarette smoke. I sat there for a while, as students came and went, listening to the rhythms of the conversations in Arabic and smiling at the familiarity of the ones in English.

'When will we have our exams back, Miss Lynn?'

'Well, when I finish marking them.'

'Please, Miss, when will this be?'

I had been told that a young Canadian called Ben was teaching in the department for a year. He arrived looking harassed and trailing a gaggle of students, who were all speaking to him at once. Ben was tall, with blonde, spiky hair. He was wearing a smart shirt and jeans, and a pair of dark glasses. He sat at a desk just in front of me and we introduced ourselves. Then he turned his attention to the students.

'I want to ask you about my essay,' said a young woman, who was leaning anxiously over the desk towards him. Ben was rummaging in his bag. He pulled out her work and held it up to her. 'This essay?' She nodded, smiling.

He tore it in half.

'But Dr. Ben, I worked hard.'

'It's not funny,' he said. She was still smiling. 'Why give me an essay where the whole thing is copied from the internet? In the States, you would get thrown out of school for this.'

On the *servees* back to Jerusalem, I sat next to a boy called Khalid, who had been in one of Ahmed's classes. I was still thinking about Ben's encounter with his student, which I had found confusing. I had sympathy for Ben, and for the worries that were written across his forehead. But I also felt there were signals in the situation that he might have been misreading. It was hard for me to tell. Khalid chatted to me about his degree. He spoke with a slight American accent, and he explained to me that he had spent a year studying in the States. About halfway through the journey, we came to a checkpoint and we all had to get out of the *servees*. As we queued up, Khalid whispered: 'They'll be nice to you. They don't want you to think they treat us like dogs.'

Al-Quds University was founded in the 1970s out of a women's college and three schools, which taught Islamic theology, nursing, and science and technology. The last of the

19

four was based in Abu Dis. Sari Nusseibeh, who became president of the university in 1995, records his early impressions in his autobiography, *Once Upon a Country*:

> The student body was, [to] quote from Kant, a crooked piece of timber that I now had to straighten out. These students embodied the radical ideological break between my generation and that of the students. Bearded fanatics, energised by the spirit of Hamas, allowed for no intellectual freedom, and those who tried to introduce some found themselves under constant harassment. People were terrified to speak their minds freely [...] The four colleges operated more like technical schools, without a humanities program and hence without the freedom of ideas that tend to break up ossified thinking. Rote learning was the norm at Al-Quds, a parrot-like repetition of facts closely aligned with social conformity.

Sari Nusseibeh is a philosopher who trained in Oxford. By the time I first visited in 2011, there were courses in History, Arabic Language and Literature, Development Studies, Geography and Media Studies. The university had small American and European Studies programmes and had recently opened a comparable centre in Israeli Studies. There was also a partnership college with the US liberal arts school, Bard College. When I arrived for the semester in 2013, Al-Quds Bard, a liberal arts college with about 400 students, was due to see its first students graduate at the end of the semester.

Yet there were also evident tensions between Palestinian and Western influences. I was told that some families were suspicious of a 'liberal' college like Al-Quds Bard. One male student told me that the girls there had become too 'kissy-kissy' with one another. My first glimpse of Al-Quds Bard would be a tall student standing outside it wearing a beret, like an extra from a 1980s high school movie. Later a member of staff told me that many of the faculty members were uneasy about the partnership with Bard 'but we know why we have to support it'. Some of the tensions were between a Palestinian elite, who were comfortable with Western influence, and others who wanted to preserve a more distinct national identity, whether religious or secular. There was visible support for Hamas and other conservative factions among a minority of students, and this seemed in part to be an expression of frustration with outside influences.

There was still a tendency towards rote learning by 2013, although not a universal one and faculty members had varied experiences and perspectives. I was to discover the benefits of a different training. My students had an extraordinary capacity to retain information. They also had a different relationship to the texts they were reading. I started to realise that the English literary tradition is intrinsically Protestant not only in content, but also in mode. We are used to books as things that we consume and internalise privately. In *Memoirs of a Leavisite*, a book that chronicles the formative period of university literary study in the 1930s to 1950s, David Ellis writes: 'Concentrating as we did on reading and sometimes re-reading a particular text, we were like nothing so much as the early Protestants let loose for the first time on the translated Bible and struggling to work out its meanings, regardless of Church authority.' In contrast, my students at Al-Quds had been taught to memorise and recite texts, including the Qu'ran. Perhaps this is why a performance text, like a Shakespeare play, was ultimately more rewarding to teach at Al-Quds than prose fiction. The students were not used to being asked about their own response to a literary work. But they were capable of making sophisticated connections between the form and style of a varied range of poems, stories and plays.

From the main gate of the campus in Abu Dis, the first thing you see is the Wall. It was built in 2002 and it was set to cut the campus in half, until there was a carefully coordinated protest. If you stand on the road, Jerusalem appears as a thin line, with the dome of the Al-Aqsa Mosque at its centre, caught between the horizon above and the Wall below. The city should be a 20-minute drive away, but it takes students who live there up to an hour and a half to get to class. The Wall highlights a uniquely difficult set of circumstances for Al-Quds, which is the Arabic name for Jerusalem. Al-Quds is the only Palestinian university not recognised by Israel's Council for Higher Education, because it maintains campuses in both Jerusalem and the West Bank. As a consequence, it can register neither as a 'foreign' institution nor as an Israeli one. For a Jerusalem-based student, this means that his or her degree is not recognised in Israel—so, for example, if you qualify as a doctor at Al-Quds but live in Jerusalem, your only option is to move abroad to use your degree.

One of my colleagues later told me about a small exchange the English Department had set up with a university in Italy. 'The idea was that faculty could come here, and we went on a visit to them. A couple of our students went to study there for a semester. When the Italian students went to the Israeli embassy to ask for a visa to come here, they were told: "There is no such university."'

At the end of my trip in 2011, I went for dinner with my relatives. Only when I looked up the address they had given me did I realise that Giv'at Ze'ev was a settlement. It is in territory that is recognised under international law as part of the West Bank, but which is just a few kilometres north of Jerusalem and is treated as a suburb of the city. The journey felt as though it was through a film set, along highways that ploughed through undeveloped land and which were occasionally framed by a fence or a section of the Wall. I did not tell my family about my visit to Al-Quds. I was meeting some of my cousins for the first time and I wasn't sure how they would react. I still felt unsure about my own view of the situation, and I did not want the whole visit to be dominated by my excursion into the West Bank.

When they drove me home, Ofer, my cousin, and his girlfriend, Devi, took me for a drink in Jerusalem. It was a warm evening, and we sat in a bar that opened out on to the street. I had shaved my head just before I left for Israel and baldness gave me a superficial resemblance to Ofer. Perhaps hidden just out of sight was the thought that if my grandparents had emigrated to Israel, I might have grown up alongside him.

'It actually changed my view of things,' Ofer told me. 'Mum moved to Giv'at Ze'ev, and when the shops were shut on a Saturday, I would have to go down to the next Arab village to get petrol, or to go to a shop. And I started to think that maybe what I had been told was not true. The Arabs I met didn't want to kill us.

'It's different for Mum's generation, and for my grandparents. They had a sense of purpose: they were building a country. But for us....'

The conversation was interrupted by the barman who, after he had realised I was English, spoke to Ofer briefly in Hebrew. 'He asks if you're going to move here,' Ofer said to me, chuckling. It was not the only time that I was asked by an Israeli if I had considered emigrating. As the country has become dominated by more religious and orthodox traditions, the traditional 'left' has become isolated and it is keen to encourage secular liberal Jews to emigrate from Europe and America.

Devi had lived in the States for ten years and her perspective seemed gently at odds with Ofer's. She told me that her mother volunteered for a charity that helped Palestinians in the West Bank travel to Israel for medical care. I was going to ask her about it, but something in the story prompted Ofer to remember an anecdote. 'When I was in the army, we were working on a checkpoint, and a woman came through who was about nine months pregnant. When we searched her, it turned out that it wasn't a baby, it was explosives.' He turned slightly towards Devi.

Ofer went to the toilet and Devi said quietly: 'That's the most he's talked about politics in years.'

# 3

# This mad reality

Murshid had a neat beard and white hair, which bristled along the back and sides of his head. I had met him on my first visit to Al-Quds. Now he had spotted me in the office, in my first week as a lecturer, and settled down to talk. He leant forward in his seat and his eyes and lips twitched, as if he was teasing me. 'Why do we make them study literature? Do you think it helps them to learn the language?' Murshid taught English language and Arabic-English translation. He had studied in the UK and, like many of the other lecturers, he spoke perfect English.

I had learnt quickly that the literature element of the degree was unpopular, and that for some lecturers and students the point was to learn to speak and write in English. Murshid suggested that the degree was poorly structured, and that students should only study literature as a part of their final year, once they had learnt enough of the language. 'But the ministry sees graduates only in terms of the number of people needed to do this or that. They don't really think about these things.' It seemed the university itself had relatively little control over the syllabus.

The semester had been delayed, and I had spent some time with Ahmed in Ramallah. One morning, we sat in the window seat of a coffee shop that perched over one of the central streets in town, and he pointed out that the shops were less crowded than usual, because most people were short of money. Israel had withheld some of the tax revenues it collects on behalf of the Palestinian Authority after the Palestinian bid for statehood at the UN in late 2012. The lecturers at Al-Quds had only received 50% of their salary for December, and this reduction was expected to continue for three months. Other public servants were in a similar position or worse. Ahmed explained that only 4,000 of the 13,000 students at the university had registered for the semester as a consequence. He predicted that there were likely to be further strikes.

As we walked around town, Ahmed told me about his family. His three sons from his first marriage lived with him. His new wife was pregnant, and he told me that he was hoping it would be a girl. Ahmed said he was planning to buy some land just outside Ramallah and build a house. As we walked around town, he pointed out that from some of Ramallah's main streets you can see out of the city to Israeli settlements. I knew that Giv'at Ze'ev must be one of them.

While we were waiting for term to start, I was asked to help invigilate an exam for students who had failed a course in the previous semester. It was in a large tiered lecture theatre and, once it was under way, I ambled up and down the steps, trying to get glimpses of the papers. One student was writing a short essay on the meaning of 'ekphrasis', a phrase (for writing inspired by art) which I had only come to understand as a young lecturer at Bristol, when one of my colleagues was writing a book about it. I could see that some of the students were struggling. One of the men had reproduced fragments that he had memorised, such as the title of Keats's poem 'Ode on a Grecian Urn' and technical terms such as 'metaphor' and 'simile'. He had misspelt both words, as if these were fish he had just caught hold of, plucked out of a sea of language he did not understand.

When I stood at the back of the lecture theatre, I could see the rows of students hunched over their desks in a familiar exam posture, writing furiously. I turned and looked out of the window. In a field, just down the hill, there was a shepherd, crouched down on his haunches, his back arched in the same way as the students. He was perched at the top of a slope and about a dozen sheep were clustered in the space below him.

Ahmed was also invigilating, and so was Fu'ad, a former

member of the English Department who now ran the university's alumni office. Fu'ad circled the lecture theatre with me, commentating in a stage whisper on the students we passed: 'This one, she's an excellent student,' or, 'This one, he is no good!' When I made my escape and sat at the front, he boomed out: 'This is your lecturer from England! You must welcome him!'

Fu'ad had been an athlete in his youth, but now he was portly and moved mostly in a shuffle. Once, in his office, he showed me a powder he was taking for weight loss. When Fu'ad spoke, his whole body would grapple with the story, his mouth curling downwards with disgust or amusement. He would clap his hands in delight at the punch line to a joke. He lived in al-Bireh, the town next to Ramallah, and so I would spend quite a bit of time with him and Ahmed, who were friends. Fu'ad had taught at the university for over twenty years. Once, as we walked around the market, we were stopped every few yards. 'He's a former student of mine,' Fu'ad would explain afterwards, before providing a brief biography of the person who had spoken to him, who was now a teacher or a judge or a businessman. Fu'ad explained that it was an essential politeness to stop and greet one another in this way.

Ahmed was always enthusiastic about my presence in the department, while Omar had been teasingly sceptical. Fu'ad was protective. 'If anyone asks you about politics,' he told me, 'Just say you do not have an opinion. Say that you are not a political person.' We were sitting in Fu'ad's office before the exam as he said this, drinking coffee. Ahmed laughed. 'He is laughing because I am a very political person,' Fu'ad confessed.

I was sitting in the office, making notes on what I had seen in the exam and trying to plan out my first class, when a group of students burst in. They stood apart from me, talking in Arabic. Later, my students were scrupulous about not speaking in Arabic, unless one of them translated. Once, when a man did offer an aside to the room, several students interjected to explain what he had said. Now, one of the young men finally broke off and came to speak to me. He was tall and looked slightly older than the others. He declared proudly that he had graduated and I congratulated him. 'I like the way Dr. Ahmed teaches,' he told me. I could not tell whether this was a welcome or a warning. I looked up at him, feeling cornered. He was smiling. 'He *teaches* — he is didactic, whereas some of the other teachers use the American way, they expect students to find out for themselves.'

One of the students who appeared was Tariq, who on my earlier visit had said that it was all a waste of time. 'Hello, doctor!' he greeted me. I tried to explain that I didn't have a PhD. Tariq looked puzzled. (I soon gave up explaining this, as the students called all of the male teachers 'doctor' and the female lecturers 'miss'.) Tariq stood slightly to the side of the desk and he spoke with his hands out, smiling. 'Which courses are you teaching, doctor?' he asked.

'Shakespeare and a course called Special Topics,' I said.

'Ah, you're teaching a seminar unit?'

'No,' I said, pointing to a list of modules that was pasted on the wall beside my desk. 'I think it's called Special Topics.'

'Ah!' he replied, and I could see him making an effort. 'But 'seminar' is the *street* name.'

Most of the students who were drifting in and out of the office seemed to be there to complain. A lecturer explained that many of them were unhappy with the courses they were taking, while one or two were protesting about having to re-take an exam. I surfed the wave of enthusiasm that came with being a newcomer, feeling that all of this did not have to be my concern. One woman, who I hadn't met before, came in to speak with me and told me that she liked English as a subject but that she didn't like the department.

'If you were head of the department, what would you change about it?' I asked, hoping she would an offer an insight I could use in my preparation.

She thought for a second and then spoke in a deep, even tone. 'I would close it,' she said.

\* \* \*

There were still problems with students registering, so only 13 out of 30 showed up for the first Shakespeare class. I asked the students who had come whether they were excited about the course. A young man called Adel, dressed in a stylish t-shirt and with hair gelled in a precise slope across his forehead, said he had taken the course before but had failed it because he found the language too difficult. A tall woman called Noor, who spoke confidently but looked shyly up under her hijab, said she had studied the sonnets and that she liked the ones about the dark lady, and that an ugly woman could be beautiful in a poem.

I had worried about how to pitch the opening class, because I assumed the students would find the language difficult. But it helped that a couple of them had seen the Baz Luhrmann film version of *Romeo and Juliet* ('We like the actor,' one woman said). We read the start of the balcony scene until just before Romeo reveals himself. The students immediately said that Romeo's speeches were easier to understand, and they spotted how he piles metaphors on metaphors to idealise Juliet. They were sceptical about Romeo. They talked about him as 'sensitive' and they knew this word, although not the word 'sulk', which I used to describe him and then had to mime.

I gave the students a handout, as most of them did not yet have a copy of the play. For each course, students would be required to buy a 'reader' from the university bookshop. This was a small centre full of photocopiers, in the basement of one of the main buildings on campus. I had taken my copies of *Romeo and Juliet* and *Julius Caesar* to them alongside a brief course outline, and they had produced a pack out of the material, enlarged so that the footnotes were more readable and with generous margins at the sides so that students could take notes. Students would then buy these bootlegged copies of the plays for their classes.

The first quotation on the handout was by a British critic, Jonathan Bate:

> Shakespeare's birthday is celebrated annually in Germany; there is a Globe Theatre in Tokyo; a library devoted to him stands on Capitol Hill in Washington, DC [in the United States]... Why has a sixteenth-century dramatist of humble origins become the best known and most admired author in the history of the world? And, anyway, what exactly *is* so special about his works?

I told the students that, although Shakespeare was now read all over the world, they should not take for granted that his works were great or special. Their job, as readers, was to discover whether he seemed like a great writer to them.

Alongside Bate's introduction, I gave the students an article by Amir Nizar Zuabi, part of a series in which people of different nationalities wrote about Shakespeare in *The Guardian*. Zuabi is a Palestinian director and actor, who has worked with the Royal Shakespeare Company. He suggests that 'the rhythms' of Shakespeare's writing are familiar to a Palestinian reader: 'For Arabs, the poetic form of the Qur'an is one of our cultural foundations, and Shakespeare's blend of verse and prose seems as natural as the way we think; it is the way we breathe.' But his larger argument is about 'what Shakespeare writes about':

> There are not a lot of places where the absolute elasticity of mankind is more visible than in the Palestinian territories. In the span of one day, you might find [yourself] reading a book in the morning, then in the afternoon be involved in what feels like a full-scale war; by dinner you and your wife have a

lengthy discussion about the quality of that book, and just before you slip into bed there is still time to witness another round of violence before you tuck the children into bed. This mad reality blends everything—injustice with humour, anger with grace, compassion with clairvoyance, comedy with tragedy. For me this is the essence of Shakespeare's writing; and the essence, too, of being Palestinian. This Shakespeare, I grant, is not an academic chap. He is Shakespeare as I think he should be performed—untamed, not civilised and polite, but alive and kicking. He lived in dangerous times, and made the most of them in his work.

The students said relatively little about the article and I could not judge what they made of it. It was also hard to get all of them to speak. The discussion ended up being dominated by the few men and a couple of the bolder women. The space didn't help. We were packed into a small room, with the students in rows facing me.

There was one student I noticed in this class, although I couldn't have said why. He was sitting in the back row and looked a little older than the other men, who seemed more like boys. He had a full beard and thick black hair sculpted in a wave above his head. He was wearing thick-rimmed black glasses. I noticed him in part because I knew he was attending to what I was saying. He sat straight-backed, almost still, but occasionally a smile played around his lips. Later, I found out that his name was Haytham.

As the material we had to work with became thinner, because they had not yet read the play, my improvisations became more desperate. We talked about the kind of actors they would cast for the main parts. I asked them who could play the Prince and, when they were silent, I kneeled down:

'Could it be a short man?'

'No!' they roared.

I put on a reedy high-pitched voice: 'Could it be me if I spoke like this?'

One woman came up to me after class and asked if we could act the play. 'There is a theatre at the university,' she said, 'but nobody uses it.'

Mundhir, one of the men from the class, walked with me to the Special Topics seminar. He told me I had to understand that the students were shy about speaking English in front of me. I wondered if group work might help, or asking the students to work in pairs. But I also feared this might degenerate into chaos, with so many students in each class. I was also wondering how to learn so many names.

Mundhir went off to his next class and nobody turned up for mine. Before I arrived, I had been told that my second course would be on the nineteenth-century novel, and I had brought with me various texts including Dickens's *A Christmas Carol*. But it turned out that I would be teaching Special Topics instead, a course for which I could select any texts. I had a limited selection of books with me. I had brought a couple of anthologies of nineteenth-century short stories, which I had hoped to use to supplement the core texts I had chosen, and I decided to focus on those instead. It was a lucky accident. In retrospect, it is hard for me to imagine how we would have ploughed through those long novels. Focusing on the short stories allowed us to move on quickly if one story didn't work, and to disappear down side-avenues between the texts.

While I was waiting in the classroom, I stood facing the window. The Shakespeare class was in a room at the very bottom of campus. But the room for this class was in the Faculty of Arts, about halfway up the hill. From the window you could see out and over the next building, beyond campus. The Wall ran horizontally across the horizon. As I was staring out of the window, a couple of students arrived and told me that the English students were all on strike 'because of the department's policies.'

As I walked back to the office, I ran into Lynn, an American woman who taught literature, and who I had met on my earlier visit. She was always slightly nervous-looking, with piercing eyes and a mischievous smile.

'I've been making lists for you,' she said, 'Need-to-know lists: how to ask for groceries in Arabic and that sort of thing. How's it going?'

'Everything's been going really well so far.'

She laughed. 'That won't last.'

We walked up a steep set of steps, back to the English Department offices, which were at the top of campus. We had to stop a couple of times, as Lynn caught her breath: 'I'm a smoker,' she apologised.

'Why are you here?' she asked me, as we stopped about halfway up. She smiled: 'I've given up being polite.'

Lynn complained that teaching at Al-Quds had become like a game of 'monkey in the middle', that the students were not interested in learning but only wanted to pass and get their grades. She said that plagiarism was rife and that students were constantly bartering for better grades. 'About 10% of the students are *really* good,' she said. 'The others are only here because....' She shrugged.

When we got back to the department, there was a throng of students in the hallway. A woman called Salwa came to apologise because she had been absent from my Shakespeare class. She mumbled nervously at first, but I understood gradually what she was saying. The *servees* she was in had been stopped at a checkpoint on the way in, and all of the students had been searched, so she had arrived too late for class. Two other women spoke to Lynn. As we turned to walk into the department, Lynn said that on her way in she had seen five Israeli armoured jeeps down the road. The students had told her that tear gas had now been set off in the town.

'Stay inside, girls,' Lynn called out over her shoulder.

# 4

# I was part of the story

Khalid and I greeted one another like old friends. He had returned home after studying in England for a year. One of the challenges, he said, was learning not to queue again. He described waiting politely in line at the Allenby Crossing from Jordan into the West Bank, only to find that everyone else surged forward. Khalid had started a Masters in Leeds shortly after we had met on the *servees* in 2011, during my first visit to the campus at Al-Quds. We had stayed in touch and he had been to visit me in Bristol. As he told me about Allenby, we were standing in a small crush of students outside one of the huts on campus where you could buy lunch. Khalid raised his hand above the heads in front of us and fixed his eyes on one of the men behind the counter. When he got the man's attention, he ordered two falafel sandwiches.

I asked Khalid to tell me more about what the degree had been like when he was a student. Murshid was not the only one with doubts about whether we should be teaching English literature. I was aware of uneasy parallels between what I was doing and the subject's history as part of the curriculum in colonial settings. Kamau Brathwaite, a poet and critic from Barbados, has written about the legacies of an English education system in the Caribbean:

> People were forced to learn things which had no relevance to themselves. Paradoxically, in the Caribbean (as in many other 'cultural disaster' areas) [...] we are more excited by [English] literary models, by the concept of, say, Sherwood Forest and Robin Hood than we are by Nanny of the Maroons, a name some of us didn't even know until a few years ago. And in

terms of what we write [...] we haven't got the syllables, the syllabic intelligence, to describe the hurricane, which is our own experience, whereas we can describe the imported alien experience of the snowfall.

I was unsure of the relevance of much of what we were going to read to my students, and I feared that they were partly resistant because learning English gave them few opportunities to articulate their own experiences.

In the Shakespeare class, we had just read the party scene at the Capulet house, at the end of Act I, in which Romeo and Juliet first catch sight of one another. The lovers speak a sonnet between them, at the end of which they kiss, not yet knowing one another's name. Only the audience knows the danger they are in. There was a subtle tension in the classroom, with some of the students shifting uncomfortably in their seats. I did not know whether I was challenging local etiquette, to suggest that two unmarried teenagers might kiss, or drawing attention to behaviour they were familiar with but embarrassed to talk about. The students had disappeared around a corner in their experience.

We skipped ahead to look at the scene in which the Nurse returns from speaking with Romeo, to establish his intentions:

Nurse: Your love says, like an honest gentleman, and a courteous and a kind, and handsome, and I warrant, a virtuous—Where is your mother?
Juliet: Where is my mother? Why, she is within.
Where should she be? How oddly thou repliest!
"Your love says, like an honest gentleman,
'Where is your mother?'"

There were ripples of laughter. It felt like a small breakthrough, although I did not know how much the silent majority among the students was taking in.

As we ate lunch in the sunshine, I told Khalid about the scene with the Nurse. 'That sounds like my grandma,' he said. 'When I go to see her in Nablus, she will tell three or four stories very quickly. You know, it took me a while to adjust to the English way of writing, that you make a point, back it up, give some evidence and so on, because in Arabic culture you go a long way round to the point. It's a completely different style.'

Khalid had a meeting in the American Studies department about a possible job as a teaching assistant. I waited outside while he was talking to one of the academics. In the hallway, there was a simple wooden frame, with eight photographs in it. They showed Barack Obama, then a senator, visiting the university in 2006. When Khalid emerged from the meeting, he told me he was uncertain whether to take the job. He was in two minds about trying to go abroad again, which was the only option if he wanted to do a PhD. He said that of his close friends from university, one had gone abroad to study dentistry, one had become a hairdresser, and one had studied business and was now working in a sweet shop. Khalid had been fired up by Paulo Freire's *Pedagogy of the Oppressed* and he thought it was important to develop ideas that were uniquely Palestinian. 'I felt like a capitalist writing my thesis,' he said. 'Why do we always say the private sector might be a good thing?' Khalid said that students in Palestine were not used to being asked 'What do you think?' or 'Do you like it or not?'

Sooner or later, when I was with Khalid, the talk would turn to a girl he had met. 'There's this girl,' he would say, before describing how he had met her or why she was just out of reach. Each time we met, there would be someone new. He was thinking aloud, and told me that he thought this new girl might be the one for him. 'You know, I can imagine it. Except that monogamy seems like a... a....'

'A nightmare?' I offered.

'One thing in England, Tom. In my circle of friends, all they wanted to do was go drinking and dancing. There isn't the same culture of *talking* in England. Nobody there wants to talk about politics—I mean, nobody wanted to talk about *British* politics, let alone Palestine.' He asked me whether I was travelling around much while I was in the West Bank. 'Have you been to Tel Aviv?' I said that I might go another time. 'I envy you so much. You can just *go*.'

One of the peculiarities of my early days on campus was how familiar some of the university routines felt, even when I found myself straining at the limits of what else I could understand. My first glimpse of Al-Quds Bard felt especially familiar. Although it is on the same campus as the main university, its buildings are newer and seem consciously modelled on an American college, with glass-fronted offices and teaching rooms. Even the students hanging around outside the building were more Western in dress. When I went to meet the Dean of the college, to discuss teaching I might do there, he told me about a letter he was opening, which confirmed that he would be given back power to approve students transferring between courses; such decisions had been briefly transferred to a more senior academic. The little tensions of academic politics were familiar from home.

I ran into Lynn during the lunch break. She asked me what students were like in Bristol, and whether we had the same problems with discipline at English universities. I said that there were problems with plagiarism and that in lectures I'd had to tell students off for talking or texting. About an hour later, I was still in the office and she came in and asked if she could wait for Ahmed. I slowly twigged that something was wrong. It was 2.30pm, and her class was due to run for another hour. She told me she had walked out because the students wouldn't listen and had refused to take a quiz she was giving them, which was a punishment for not having had the texts with them in the previous class. We talked a little, and Ahmed arrived with the president of the students' English Club and Haytham, the student I had spotted in my Shakespeare class. I had discovered that the English Club existed mainly to negotiate with staff. The students Lynn was teaching were second years, and they did not always understand English. Haytham turned to me and explained that in the first year, the students took general courses and intensive language lessons only began in the second year. Most of the students I was teaching were in the fourth year. Lynn asked if the students found her difficult to understand because of her accent and Haytham said that wasn't a problem.

'The thing is,' Lynn said, after they left. 'I have no children and I never taught high school. I have no experience of disciplining kids.'

We did not have the first Special Topics class until about two weeks into term. Lynn and I were scheduled in the same room, with many of the same students, so we all met at the department to resolve it. Lynn agreed to come in early to teach her course, because she lived closer to campus. I still had an hour with the class afterwards and we read the first of the short stories, 'An Arrest' by Ambrose Bierce, which is about a fugitive called Orrin Brower. It is only two pages long. I asked the students to point out any words they did not know. There were about twenty of them, including buckshot, fugitive, aching, and captor. Shortly after escaping, Brower gets lost, but he is determined to keep walking for as long as he can: 'Even an added hour of freedom was worth having.' He is apprehended and led back to prison by a gaoler:

Brower was as courageous a criminal as ever lived to be hanged; that was shown by the conditions of awful personal peril in which he had coolly killed his brother-in-law. It is needless to relate them here; they came out at his trial, and the revelation of his calmness in confronting them came near to saving his neck. But what would you have? --when a brave man is beaten, he submits.

The students debated whether Brower was courageous or not, since he had committed a crime. Someone said that Brower had killed his brother-in-law, which made him a bad person, whereas others emphasised the mysterious 'conditions of awful personal peril' in which he had done it. I texted Lynn later to thank her. She replied: 'Happy to help. By the way, this was once a very different place. So sorry you could not have come when we still had a chance of making this a first-rate school.'

Early on, we also read 'A Toy Princess' by Mary De Morgan, a children's tale, in which there is a land where the people are without emotions. The king marries a foreign woman, who dies shortly after the birth of their daughter. The baby princess infuriates everyone by crying and is rescued by a fairy godmother. She is replaced with a 'toy princess', who can only say a series of polite phrases: 'just so', 'yes indeed', 'thank you' and 'if you please'. I asked if the story would be different if it was called 'A Toy Prince' and one woman said emphatically that this was a description of how girls were expected to behave in Palestine, to be good and polite, whereas boys could be noisy and misbehave. Wafa said that the story was disappointing because society did not want to change. When the secret is revealed, the king and his followers choose to keep the toy princess instead of the real one.

There were fewer men than women in this class and the men would often sit together at the back. Whereas any sign of touching between the sexes was taboo, the men were strikingly physical with one another. They sometimes greeted one another with a kiss on each cheek, and they would sit in class with an arm over one another's shoulder, or tap a friend on the thigh to make a point. Haytham had swapped to the Special Topics course. Students often shifted about in the early part of term, to get into the courses they wanted or so they would have enough credits for the semester. One of the men had been trying to make a point but struggling to articulate it. 'What he is trying to say,' Haytham said, 'is that the wrong person always gets rewarded. It's like in Egypt, the wrong person ends up in power, by accident or because they have no passion and so nobody is afraid of them.'

\* \* \*

One afternoon in the staff room, I talked to Lynn about writers we were both interested in and I mentioned the Sufis, a mystical branch of Islam that had influenced Ted Hughes and Doris Lessing. Lynn warned me that the Sufis were controversial for some sects within Islam. She explained that she had been asked to teach religion and mythology because she was a Christian, so could remain outside such disputes. (Later, Lynn told me that she had converted to Judaism and moved to Israel nearly thirty years earlier and had taught in Israeli universities before coming to Al-Quds.)

I forgot about this conversation. As we were speaking, the photocopier jammed while it was churning out handouts for Lynn's class. We opened up a compartment at the end, to retrieve the lost paper and ended up with our hands covered in ink, as though we had just had our fingerprints taken. We were giggling when another lecturer came in, who Lynn introduced as Rashad. She said: 'He is *the* one who all the students respect.' Rashad was a thin man, who was dressed in a smart blazer. 'They will do anything he asks,' Lynn said. Rashad responded with a saying in Arabic and then translated it. 'Be firm, but not inflexible; bend, but do not break.'

A few weeks later, I ran into Fu'ad after class and he took me to the Faculty of Da'wa and Religious Studies. I'd told him that I was interested in finding out more about the Sufis. We met an academic called Mohammed, who said he was 'half a Sufi' and who asked us to come back in an hour. In the meantime, we dropped in to another office along the corridor, in which two men were drinking coffee and smoking. Fu'ad explained that one of them was a lecturer and the other had just been released from prison. Fu'ad said that he had taught this man 'after many years.'

The conversation was fragmented, as neither of the men spoke English. Fu'ad reported that they had not heard of Idries Shah, whose work had influenced Lessing and Hughes. Eventually I realised that the discussion was becoming tense. Fu'ad stopped translating. In the midst of a long speech, the lecturer said two words that I understood: 'Salman Rushdie'. Fu'ad started to move only sporadically into English. He suggested that people should have debated Rushdie instead of condemning him. The conversation came to an abrupt end and Fu'ad stood up. We went through the usual pleasantries on our way out, shaking hands and saying a few polite phrases in a perfunctory way. I felt embarrassed as we left and feared that I had offended the men. We went back to meet Mohammed, who rocked back in his chair, laughing, when Fu'ad explained what had happened. 'These guys *hate* the Sufis!'

\* \* \*

My conversation with Khalid became part of the first assignment I set in Special Topics. I asked the students to listen to a story being told around them, or to choose a famous spoken story they were familiar with, and to analyse it using the approach we had developed in class, paying attention to its form, the language, who was telling the story, the type of story and then giving some commentary on why they liked or disliked it. I asked them also to include three Arabic words or phrases that were important in the narrative and to translate them. My encounter in the Faculty of Da'wa and Religious Studies had made me aware of just how much I did not understand the structures and tensions of the society I was living within, not least because I could not speak Arabic. I hoped my students would teach me more about Palestine, as well as articulating their own experiences.

The stories that the students shared were a mixture of folk or fairy tales, episodes from family history, and incidents that had happened to them. I found that a few of the stories had been plagiarised from the internet. These ones tended to sound like lost tales from the *Arabian Nights* and I wondered whether the students were giving me what they thought I wanted, a generic folk tale about the Middle East.

Wafa included a story which her grandmother had told her. A young prince asks to marry his cousin, but she humiliates him by making him pick a pomegranate berry off the floor with his mouth. The prince sneaks back into the palace disguised as a poor man and sings to his cousin, who falls in love with him. She lives with him in poverty and disgrace, before he reveals himself to be the real prince. Wafa explained why she liked the story:

> I heard it when I was young and I love the ending, 'they lived happily ever after.' Some of the dialogue is presented by songs. On the one hand, it's similar to the stories which we read in class, it's a fairytale as is 'A Toy Princess'. On the other hand, it's different. The story is told in my language, it's full of terms that only Palestinians know and, most importantly, it's an oral story. Each time my grandmother Wajiha tells the story, she adds some events and omits some. Her way of storytelling hooks us immediately, the way she sings and the intonation while she imitates the characters. The story is from Palestinian folklore, it's not very famous, it's called 'Haj Brambo'. It shows how Palestinian cousins are used to getting married, especially in the previous generation. It also gives a moral that we have to think in our heart and mind, not only our heart, when we get married.

A number of the stories were about real events. A young woman called Marah wrote about an incident that had occurred in Nablus:

My grandmother told me the story when I was little. The story took place during the 1960s in Palestine, at the Turkish baths. They used firewood, timber and sawdust to heat the bathroom floor. The domes and skylight of most of the bathrooms were made of wood. Women used to go there on special occasions and before their weddings. A fire spread in the bathroom that was for women only. Usually, the women went there naked and others used to put a towel around their body. When the fire spread around the place, some women were smuggled out, but the naked women remained there out of fear and shyness. When they asked the doorman if anyone had died, he said: 'The women who were shy died' ('*Elli estaho mato*').

Marah included an aside, explaining that the phrase 'the women who were shy died' now had a wider application. She said it was used to describe a loss of modesty in Palestine; the fact that traditional religious values were not respected as they had once been.

I had asked the students to note down who had told them the story, and usually they were narrated by other family members. One of the women wrote:

My father told me this story two years ago, while we were at a picnic. In a small village near Ramallah, about 25 years ago, the Israeli soldiers broke into our house. My grandfather was the most dangerous wanted man in Palestine because he had an unwarranted weapon. The Israeli soldiers were doing raids to catch people who went against their laws. Two months later, they came again and tried to torture us to confess where he was. But no-one told them this secret, where he was hiding. Two years passed: then they caught him. The Israeli soldiers decided to execute him publicly and then hang his body in the village, so all the villagers would see him and be afraid to do what he did. My father ended the story by describing how brave and courageous my grandfather was. I like this story very much because it's realistic. This story talks about our reality and our society. It also describes our current situation. It seems that this is happening now. I also like it because my grandfather was very courageous. He protected his country and died while doing that. He was a hero, at least my family and I think that. He was not a terrorist. I'm very proud of him, because he died while he was holding his gun.

The students sometimes set the stories against key episodes in Palestinian history, as they did when they re-wrote *Romeo and Juliet*. One student wrote about a young nurse called Inas, who chose to stay in Akka in 1948 when the rest of her family had fled, because she had fallen in love with an ill man named Ramez. She was killed a few months later by invading Israeli forces, as she tried to send food to Ramez. 'Although Inas's death makes me very sad,' she wrote, 'it also established the idea that our land is the most important thing that we have.' Another student wrote a story about a 7-year old boy in contemporary Gaza, who chose to throw stones at the Israelis when he found out that they had killed his father and brother, and who was subsequently killed.

In Ruba's story, she was both the narrator and a participant:

I was a part of the story, and one of the people who actually told it many times, and also heard a lot of family members and friends telling it and talking about it. It happened on a very normal day, just like any other day, after midnight in 2005. My family and I were sitting in the living room, chatting and watching TV, about to prepare ourselves for bedtime. All of a sudden we heard someone knocking on our door and screaming: 'Open up, open up!' My father got up, opened it and in a second the whole building we live in was filled with Israeli soldiers, guns, boxes and the first thing they did, they locked all of us in the living room, put the power off, and asked us not to move or make any sound or even light a candle. A few hours later, they took my father. We had no idea where, whether he was still alive or not, and after that all we heard was gunshots, and speakers asking two guys to walk out of the house. Twelve hours passed and we did not hear anything about my father. When the morning came, my father came in, shaking, his whole body was weak and it was the first time in my life I saw tears coming down from his eyes. Suddenly, the Israeli soldiers put their guns down, started talking and joking, like none of this was happening, they finished what they came for. They killed two young men, they destroyed the entire building. It turned out the two men were wanted by the Israelis and, after they had accomplished their mission, they took my father as a human shield, to drag the bodies out. It was terrifying and it was probably the worst day of my life and the hardest to forget.

I was struck that Ruba told the story in such a straightforward way. I read it several times and I wondered what I might say to a student in England, if she reported an incident this traumatic; what my role would be as her teacher. I was glad that Ruba had written about her experience. But I also felt powerless. Ruba had taught me, among other things, what it feels like to have no part in the story.

# 5

# The rights of the reader

I had been trying to persuade Haytham to do the reading for class, so when I got an e-mail from him, after we had looked at an extract from Malcolm X's *Autobiography*, it felt like a small breakthrough:

> Regarding why do I think that reading is not necessary, the whole idea got changed after hearing Malcolm's part of the story which actually convinced me. However I would love to re-talk about [it] all on Tuesday and I think I have some cool thoughts regarding this matter.

Haytham was not the only student who often did not do the reading. Some of the students were taking six or seven classes at the same time and claimed they had too much preparatory work to do. Others saw the reading as peripheral; they wanted to come to class, write down the answers, and prepare themselves for the exam. But Haytham's resistance bothered me. He was one of the most engaged students in seminars, participating in debates with passion and humour. I could not make sense of his reluctance.

Then I met Farooq. He had lived in the UK and we'd been put in touch by mutual friends. Farooq was in his early forties. He told me he was a Bedouin and that his family was from a village in the very south of the West Bank, which was being encircled by settlements. Their original land, including an orchard, was now part of an Israeli kibbutz, just the other side of the border. Farooq had won a scholarship for refugee children and moved to England. He described his disorientation when he arrived in the UK: 'Until I was ten, I lived in tents made of goat's hair.'

Farooq had a grant to do work in the West Bank and in Gaza,

helping schools with aspects of child development and especially with reading. He showed me photographs of the fish markets in Gaza, which he had just visited, including huge crates full of crabs. He told me he had a British passport as well as a Palestinian identity card. 'The Israelis want me to give up my ID card, of course,' he said. 'It's ethnic cleansing by stealth.'

Several people had told me that reading was not part of the culture in Palestine. Farooq was dismissive. 'I've heard that a lot—it's nonsense,' he said 'It's to do with deprivation, not culture. I don't read a lot because I grew up in an illiterate culture, whereas my wife always has two, three, four books on the go.' Farooq was involved in setting up a project to encourage young people to read. But, like many people I met in Ramallah, he had become sceptical about development, because it was becoming an 'industry' with the proliferation of NGOs in the West Bank.

Farooq's response emboldened me. In one of the next Special Topics classes, I asked the students why they did not read. A couple of students said they preferred films or computer games. Another student said that he did not like reading because it meant not taking any action. One of the women said she preferred spoken stories. Salwa talked about how some books were threatening to her religious beliefs, and Nazeeha said she stopped reading a book if she did not like the way it made her think. A student called Tamam cited a lack of time, because of his job. He was working fulltime to help open a shop, while also trying to complete his degree. (Towards the end of the semester, he was lucky to escape unscathed from a fire at the shop.)

I asked the students to imagine what life would be like if you could not read at all. This was an exercise I had sometimes used at home, with mature students who were being asked to set up a reading group in the community. I would ask them to create two fictional characters, a reader and a non-reader: 'Just think: if you could not read *at all*,' I said, repeating a line I had used in seminars in Bristol, 'you would not be able to read what was for sale in a shop, or on a street sign....' Tariq interrupted me, good-humouredly: 'But here there are no signs for anything!'

The discussion about why one would read was a little slower. Haytham was sharp in asking about the distinction between being *able* to read and choosing to read *literature*. He noted that to learn a language, one only needs to speak it, and he gave the example that many Palestinians working in Israel could speak Hebrew fluently, but could not read it. This brought us to the perennial concern among the students that reading literature was irrelevant to learning the English language.

I gave the students an extract from Malcolm X's *Autobiography*, in which he describes his growing awareness of his illiteracy while in prison: 'I became increasingly frustrated at not being able to express what I wanted to convey in letters that I wrote, especially those to Mr. Elijah Muhammad. In the street, I had been the most articulate hustler out there.' He starts to copy out the dictionary, and ultimately becomes an obsessive reader. He is outraged by the prison's policy of putting the lights out at 10pm: 'It always seemed to catch me right in the middle of something engrossing.'

> Fortunately, right outside my door was a corridor light that cast a glow into my room. The glow was enough to read by, once my eyes adjusted to it. So when "lights out" came, I would sit on the floor where I could continue reading in that glow. At one-hour intervals the night guards paced past every room. Each time I heard the approaching footsteps, I jumped into bed and feigned sleep. And as soon as the guard passed, I got back out of bed onto the floor area of that light-glow, where I would read for another fifty-eight minutes—until the guard approached again. That went on until three or four every morning. Three or four hours of sleep a night was enough for me.

Malcolm X concludes the account by saying that reading 'awoke inside me some long dormant craving to be mentally alive.' We talked about the opposite of being 'mentally alive,' and Adel suggested it would mean being a 'zombie.'

I had given the students a few other quotations about reading, one of which was a remark attributed to Einstein: 'Somebody who only reads newspapers and at best books of contemporary authors looks to me like an extremely near-sighted person who scorns eyeglasses. He is completely dependent on the prejudices and fashions of his times.' Tariq linked this to Malcolm X's claim that he read primarily those works that would help 'the black man': 'Isn't he near-sighted too, because he is always reading for a purpose?' Haytham, who up until this point had seemed openly sceptical, said that Malcolm X read in order to have power. After class, one woman came up to me and said she thought this was not quite right. She suggested that he had read, and written, in order to lead.

That afternoon, Lynn arrived in the office, tearful, having again walked out of a class. She told me that she had been having problems getting students to buy books, so she had made all the material available online this time, which they also complained about. She had already spoken to Ahmed about it and I offered to walk her down the road to the *servees*. When we got to the front gate of campus, I said that the students wanted to get under her skin and she shouldn't let them and I encouraged her to go home and enjoy the sunshine.

'What did you do about the books?' I asked, as she turned to leave.

'I didn't do anything,' she replied. She explained that the Hamas student group had paid to print out copies of the material she had posted online.

\* \* \*

Haytham spoke first. In the next class, I gave out a copy of a 'Bill of Rights' for readers, by the French novelist Daniel Pennac:

1.  The right to not read
2.  The right to skip pages
3.  The right to not finish
4.  The right to reread
5.  The right to read anything
6.  The right to escapism
7.  The right to read anywhere
8.  The right to browse
9.  The right to read out loud
10. The right to not defend your tastes

I asked the students what they would add to or remove from Pennac's list. Haytham said: 'In Palestine, the first thing you would need is the right to not be arrested—for what you read, or for what you do with what you read.' In the discussion that followed, students said that this would once have applied to the way in which the Israelis behaved, but they were now also afraid of the Palestinian Authority.

Inas queried 'the right to read out loud.' She said this might annoy other people, which provoked a discussion about the balance in rights, between the individual and the effect on others. Someone said that you *should* have to defend your tastes; otherwise you could say something hateful and get away with it. Another student, laughing, said there should be a right 'not to be interrupted,' so she could always say to her mother that she could not do something else if she was reading. Tariq said you should have the right to add to what you read, to write, and to 'protect' what you read, by which he meant the ideas, not the physical book. We looped back to Haytham's point, and got to the 'right *to* read' and someone else said you should have the right to 'criticise what you read.' Pennac made the reader important, the students noted, giving him or her power, which might normally rest with the author.

After class, a student called Anwar trailed me back up to the office. He had spent a couple of weeks volunteering with a charity in England in the summer of 2012. He said he was surprised by how many very poor, even homeless, people there were in London. He also said he had found people materialistic and that people drank in order to talk. 'I was asked to give a presentation at a university about the situation here, and some students interrupted me.'

'What did they say?' I asked.

'They said I was a terrorist.'

Our next short story was 'The Yellow Wallpaper' by Charlotte Perkins Gilman, published in 1892. While I was reading about Gilman's story, I came across a quotation from the writer Maxine Hong Kingston: 'The difference between mad people and sane people… is that sane people have variety when they talk-story. Mad people have only one story that they talk over and over.'

'The Yellow Wallpaper' is in the form of a diary written by a woman who has been confined to a house that has been rented for the summer by her husband, John, while she recuperates from depression. John is a doctor and he has forbidden his wife from writing, so she has to hide the journal entries from him. She becomes obsessed with the patterns and colour of the wallpaper in her room and is convinced there is a woman hiding behind it.

The language in the story is relatively straightforward and it seemed to touch a chord. I began by talking about what 'interpretation' means: 'to explain,' said Adel; 'to understand' someone else said. We talked about an 'interpreter' as someone who would need to understand but also explain. I pointed out both that the story was open to interpretation and that illness might be as well. We discussed whether the narrator is reliable, and why she is a writer. I listed the woman behind the wallpaper as a character and then asked: if the narrator has imagined this person, and we only have her account of anything, do we know if any of the other characters are real? There was a sharp intake of breath to my left and a couple of students jolted back slightly, as if a wave of thought had hit them.

One woman said the story was about how to treat psychological illness. Gilman herself had seen it this way, as a critique of contemporary medical practice. Someone else remarked that the narrator is a 'prisoner,' because she cannot go anywhere. 'Did she do something bad?' one student asked. She said later that John was the real prisoner because he was a victim of his own thoughts.

At the end of the class, the students made a tentative start with teaching me some Arabic. I had told them I was taking lessons in Ramallah. 'This is your chance to have revenge on me,' I said. 'This is *good*,' Inas replied. I asked Marah to come up and write 'the yellow wallpaper' on the board in Arabic. There was a dispute among the students about whether the formal or slang version was more appropriate. At one point they were all shouting different things, and I stood aside as Marah took on the role of the teacher. 'I love this,' I said, as they all shouted across one another. 'This is democracy!'

* * *

When I first arrived in the West Bank, I had a conversation with an American friend in Ramallah. I said that I had met several people in my first few weeks at the university, both staff and students, who seemed depressed. But I was unsure whether to call it depression, which is (too) often seen as an illness afflicting an individual. The unhappiness I was encountering, in contrast, seemed to be a reflection of the intractable situation in the West Bank. The occupation is brutal in many ways, but some of the most pernicious effects are subtle and cumulative. Edward Said once wrote that Zionism was effective because of its attention to *detail*. Palestinian lives are disrupted in endless small ways, day to day.

In the late 1990s, my father interviewed his mother, Lisl, about her life. He asked her what she remembered about the Nazi occupation of Vienna:

> David: So how long were you there after the Nazis came into Austria?
> Lisl: I think we left on the first or second of June [1938], something like that—and they moved in the middle of March.
> David: So what do you remember about that—about them actually being there?
> Lisl: The main thing, I really remember very vividly, is when we went through our books and burnt everything we thought with the slightest political connection or anti-.... So we had a stove and we had to burn a lot of stuff. And that was the famous occasion when we found a book that my cousin had given us to keep. He didn't say what it was. He said: 'Can you keep this for me?' and [your] father put it on our bookshelf and when he went through the books—what to get rid of—he found that. And that was a plan for street fighting of the Communist Party. If they had found that it would have been the end of us.

(In the same interview, Lisl recounted how she became a Zionist after attending a meeting in 1924, when she was sixteen. 'It just clicked with me. I was ready for something. If I had gone by chance to a Communist meeting, that would have clicked [instead].')

In his novel *Fahrenheit 451*, Ray Bradbury constructs a dystopian society, in which books are banned. The main character, Guy Montag, is a fireman, whose job is to burn books, but who gradually becomes curious about them. He becomes friends with a former English professor called Faber. 'We have everything we need to be happy, but we aren't happy,' Montag laments: 'I thought books might help.' Faber replies:

> You're a hopeless romantic. [...] It's not books you need, it's some of the things that once were in books. [...] The same infinite detail and awareness could be projected through the radios, and televisors, but are not. No, no it's not books at all you're looking for! Take it where you can find it, in old phonograph records, old motion pictures, and in old friends; look for it in nature and look for it in yourself. Books were only one type or receptacle where we stored a lot of things we were afraid we might forget. There is nothing magical in them at all. The magic is only in what books say, how they stitched the patches of the universe together into one garment for us.

Faber goes on to point out that books in themselves are of no use, unless they are books of quality ('The good writers touch life often'), and unless people have leisure to digest them and the right to carry out actions based on what they read.

I didn't manage to persuade Haytham to do all of the reading for the seminars. But it turned out he was right all along. He knew, better than I did, that it was not books that he needed.

# 6

# Storm warnings

'Tom, *salaam, keif halek?*'

I replied *'kulshi tmam,'* a phrase that would sometimes solicit a smile or a chuckle; it means 'everything's perfect.' I saw Munther wince a little as I said it. We exchanged a few more phrases of Arabic, and then he switched into English. 'One of our guys was shot,' he said, 'in the chest and near the heart.' It was lunchtime and I had gone into one of the cafés which was popular with Westerners in Ramallah. Munther, the owner, often wandered between tables, joining in with conversations and telling stories. The young man, who worked as a chef, had been at a demonstration at the Ofer prison the day before. The prison was located halfway between Ramallah and Giv'at Ze'ev.

There had been protests across the West Bank after the death of Arafat Jaradat. He had died in an Israeli prison on 19 February 2013. He was thirty. The human rights organisation, Al-Haq, reported:

> The autopsy confirmed that he was tortured. Arafat died of shock and not of a heart attack, as was initially thought. His body showed signs of beating on his chest, back and shoulders near the spine and two broken ribs. The post-mortem found blood in Arafat's nose and bruises inside his mouth.

Arafat had a pre-existing back injury, from being hit with a tear gas canister. He had been arrested for throwing stones a few days before. One report said a settler had been injured. Israel's health ministry claimed that the bruising and broken ribs were probably the result of attempts to revive him.

Munther said that the Palestinians were in limbo, not knowing what to do. 'Why does nobody do anything about the fact that we build the settlements? Why does nobody give the workers money not to?' He said the Palestinian attitude to the political situation was a mess: 'It's like an essay where every paragraph says something different.'

\* \* \*

It snowed for three days in January, just after I had arrived in Ramallah. I was living on the fifth floor of an apartment block and my bedroom was battered by storms on two sides. On the first night, something fell from the roof and smashed on the terrace outside. For a few days, I slept on the sofa, where it was quieter and warmer. One morning, I came down and a sheet of ice covered the steps at the front of the building. I tried to take a step, but it was too slippery, so I sat and slid down into the street instead.

Ramallah is a bubble in which one can sometimes blot out the worst tensions in the West Bank. It has grown rapidly. Edward Said remarked that before 1948 it had been a 'garden suburb of Jerusalem'. It has also changed from being a predominantly Christian town, to one where the majority of the population is Muslim. The Israelis have been keen to nurture Ramallah as a potential future capital of Palestine, in place of Jerusalem. It has also grown in significance because the main Palestinian cities— including Jaffa, Haifa, and much of Jerusalem—vanished into Israel. Ramallah is in Area A, the area of the West Bank that is under civil and security control by the Palestinian Authority. Most of the Westerners living in the area settle there (I was once told that there were several hundred Finnish people in the city), and it has various bars and restaurants designed to cater for them.

One of my friends in Ramallah held a weekly curry night for a while, through which I met an assortment of European and

American journalists, NGO workers and students. I started to realise that the West Bank could be a very different place as a single woman. At one of these evenings I met Sunneva, a woman from the Faroe Islands who was teaching at a refugee camp near Birzeit. 'Yesterday on the way to class, a boy—he was about ten—stood and threw stones at me. So I ignored him, but one hit me on the arm.' She showed me a small bruise on her left elbow. 'On the way back, I found as large a stone as I could, and I held it up when I passed him, and he ran away. Then a slightly older boy started walking with me. He asked what my name was and where I was going. I thought he was just being friendly and then he said that he wanted to kiss me.'

In late February, I went walking with a group of friends near a monastery called Mar Saba, close to Bethlehem. One of the girls, Nathalie, asked if we could stop in Bethlehem to collect her boyfriend, Fadi. Six of us were crammed into a small car, and we burst out of it at intervals, in high spirits. Along the way, we stopped at a sheer cliff-face that had been turned into a rubbish tip. You could see waste material clinging to the sides all the way down, and the stench pushed us away after a few minutes.

We had lunch overlooking the desert, towards Jordan, and then began a trek across lower ground, heading back towards Bethlehem. At the start of the walk, we had seen other groups of tourists. Now we were on our own, following Fadi's sense of direction. At one point we all clustered around a camel, taking photographs. Fadi said something that sounded good-humoured to Nathalie. She translated: 'He said that if you got that close to a male camel, it would swing you by the head.'

Mar Saba is on a cliff above the Kidron River, and we were making our way back towards it on the riverbed. It was a picturesque walk. The landscape was amber-beige, with the building emerging out of the rock face. Yet the dry land was punctured, here and there, with colour: a scattering of red flowers with black centres and a clutch of small yellow flowers, with long thin petals around a red centre and prickly leaves like a cactus. But the river was full of untreated wastewater, flowing from Jerusalem about 10km east. It was covered in a dirty-white foam, and the smell was incredible: it invaded your mouth before your nostrils. Initially, we all found it quite amusing. My friend Simon shouted '*zaki!*' (the Arabic for 'delicious'), and Fadi roared with laughter. After a while, we all started to feel queasy. When we finally had to cross the river, we formed a human chain across a sequence of rocks, making timid leaps across small sections of water. For the last stretch of the walk, back up the valley, Fadi skipped on ahead of us as we scrambled up a rocky climb. I could see him and Nathalie just ahead of us, laughing. I looked up and Nathalie smiled: 'He says English people don't know how to walk.'

According to the Applied Research Institute in Jerusalem (ARIJ), Israel controls up to 89% of the West Bank's water systems, and there are controls over even basic access. In Area C, which is under full Israeli control, the procedure makes it almost impossible to get planning permission to build anything, including a toilet. As a result, many people build 'illegally', only to see the structures demolished. Between 2009 and 2011, according to a 2012 article by ARIJ researchers in *This Week in Palestine*, the Israeli military demolished 173 water, sanitation and hygiene structures, including 57 rainwater collection cisterns, 40 community wells, and at least 20 toilets and sinks.

When we got back to the car, our mood revived briefly. One of the boys said: 'Well, to begin with we were relaxed and by the end we smelled of shit and feared death at any minute.' Simon smiled. 'A bit like life,' he said.

Fadi wanted to come back with us to Ramallah, but Simon — who was driving — was hesitant. We would have to pass through the checkpoint near Bethlehem. He thought we were likely to be stopped, and Fadi did not have the right permit.

\* \* \*

I asked the students why one person might kill another, and they suggested emotions such as anger, love, or jealousy. Anwar said that one might kill to get respect or power. Another student said you might kill for a 'joke.' I said that one might also kill by accident. Then we read Act III scene i. In Mercutio's speech, he lists the reasons why Benvolio has started quarrels:

> Thou hast quarrelled with a man for coughing in the street, because he hath wakened thy dog that hath lain sleeping in the sun. Didst thou not fall out with a tailor for wearing his new doublet before Easter, with another, for tying his new shoes with old riband? (III, I, 24-29)

When Mercutio is killed shortly afterwards, the text offers the instruction: 'Tybalt under Romeo's arm thrusts Mercutio in and flies.' This has been interpreted in different ways. In Franco Zeffirelli's 1968 film, for example, the scene is mostly play fighting, with both Mercutio and Tybalt trying to entertain the crowd and make one other look foolish. Tybalt is horrified to realise that he has harmed Mercutio, when he sees blood on his sword as he pulls it back under Romeo's arm.

I asked two of the men to stand up, and I positioned one as Mercutio and the other between us, as Romeo. I killed Mercutio 'under Romeo's arm,' with a whiteboard marker as a sword. I asked whether Tybalt was using Romeo as cover, and showed how he might deliberately kill Mercutio. The students were sure that, as in Zeffirelli's film, it was an accident.

During the snow days in January, I had started watching the American television series *The Wire*. I especially loved season two, about the port in Baltimore, in which a young man named Ziggy Sobotka is trying to prove himself. He is the son of a tough union leader, but he lacks his father's guile. He is subject to a series of humiliations by the other dockworkers. In a late episode in the season, called 'Storm Warnings', Ziggy finally pulls off a big deal, only to find out he has been cruelly played. He goes into a rage and shoots the man who has ripped him off. Ziggy returns to his car and we see his blood-stained hand shaking, as the siren of an ambulance or a police car sounds in the background. I found that I had tears in my eyes at the end of the episode.

I had been watching *The Wire* as a diversion and although I had been gripped by it, this was the first episode that moved me. It was only a couple of days later, walking around the market in Ramallah, that I understood why. Ziggy cannot read the codes of the adult world around him so, for example, he ends up boasting excessively if things go well. He is shocked by the reality of killing someone and, at that moment, he suddenly seems like an innocent. I saw echoes of his situation not only in Romeo and Tybalt, but also in the young men I was teaching. I could see how one of them might get caught up in the violence around him without understanding the possible consequences.

\* \* \*

Haytham's face betrayed him. 'Marriage is a problem,' he said. Several of the women turned in their seats, answering him in murmurs or declarations of dissent, and there was a ripple of emotion. But Haytham showed no pleasure at eliciting this response, as he would have done on other occasions. He raised his eyebrows slightly, as if he was baffled that others could dispute what he had said. I asked him to explain. 'It means responsibility,' he said, 'and other people having a claim on you all of the time.'

The students were starting to get the hang of having a debate in class. To begin with, they had been keen for me to tell them the right answer. For example, Guy de Maupassant's story, 'Country

Living', had seemed ideal for class discussion. The story is about two poor families, who are offered a chance to have one of their children adopted by a rich and childless couple. One family accepts and is shunned by the community as a consequence. But the adopted son returns at the end and is grateful. Marah was adamant that the parents were right to let their child be adopted. She asked her classmates to imagine that the story was about a Palestinian family letting their child live in a Gulf state. Others were equally sure that the other poor family was right to keep their child. They hastily dismissed one another's arguments, expecting me to choose a side. 'The real moral here is not to have children,' Tariq said, easing the tension.

For these students, the prospect of marriage and children was not a distant one. A number of them were married. Marah took her honeymoon during the semester, while another student asked for extra time on an assignment because of the pressure her divorce was putting her under. She was 21 and had two children. Three of my students were pregnant. According to the Palestinian Central Bureau of Statistics, the median age at which men were married in 2013 was 24.7, while women were on average 20.2 years old.

Haytham's views on marriage had been provoked by Thomas Hardy's story 'Interlopers at the Knap', which opens with a wealthy farmer, Charles Darton, travelling to meet Sally Hall, who he is due to marry. But events intervene, and he marries someone else. Much later, after his wife has died, Darton tries to woo Sally again, but she chooses to stay single. I told the students that I would read aloud the opening few paragraphs and I asked them, as with earlier stories, to underline any words they did not know. As I read, I saw the students were underlining whole sections, or staring in bewilderment at Hardy's idiosyncratic prose. 'I really *tried* to read this!' Inas said.

We read the ending together:

'Please do not put this question to me any more,' [Sally said],
'Friends as long as you like, but lovers and married never.'
'I never will,' said Darton. 'Not if I live a hundred years.'
And he never did. That he had worn out his welcome in her
heart was only too plain.
[…] It was only by chance that, years after, he learnt that Sally,
notwithstanding the solicitations her attractions drew down
upon her, had refused several offers of marriage, and steadily
adhered to her purpose of leading a single life.

The students debated whether this was a happy or a sad ending,
and most thought it was both, and that there is a sort of melan-
choly in the reference to Sally's heart. A few students speculated
that Sally was hiding a secret in her life, and Haytham said that
he thought she might have a lover. 'It's a happy ending,' he
insisted, as everyone started to get up at the end of class,
'because nobody got married.'

I had been taking Arabic lessons twice a week in Ramallah. In
one lesson, my teacher, Mohammed, taught me minutes, hours,
and days; fruits and vegetables; the numbers above ten and a
series of phrases. I had only just started to write in Arabic, so I
wrote the phrases down as I heard them.

*ana quis chukran bas ana mish mutafa-el fi falestin elyom*
I am well but I am not hopeful about Palestine today

*fi mushkile*
There are problems

*aseer*
prisoner

*asra*
prisoners

*ed-rab an e-ta-am*
The hunger strike (or 'the strike about food')

*ehna kareena kesa Thomas Hardy an zawaj*
We read a Thomas Hardy story about marriage

*ez-zawaj mushkile*
Marriage is a problem

Mohammad told me that a dowry in the West Bank was often as much as 20,000 shekels, the equivalent of about £3,000, and that it was '*mushkile*,' because people could not afford it. He also said that most boys were adamant that they did not want to get married until they were 22 or 23, and then they did.

The West Bank was tense for several weeks after Arafat Jaradat's death, with visible protests and skirmishes. I had just started to settle into a routine, and now I felt again that each day threw up something unpredictable. I had breakfast with Ahmed and Fu'ad one morning, in Fu'ad's office, and asked them how things might develop. Ahmed was adamant that the situation would not get worse; that people were too apathetic to start a third intifada, and that there would only be one if the PA collapsed. Fu'ad was more equivocal, telling me that if I died, it would be Allah's will. He said he was a believer, but not a fanatic.

I was teaching until late that day, so I ended up trying to get on a *servees* at the busiest time—about 4.30pm. One of the men who organised the rides latched on to me, and eventually he got me a seat.

On the *servees*, I got chatting to Qais. He had suddenly appeared in my Shakespeare class about eight weeks in. He was a skinny boy and slightly pale-looking. He always wore a baseball cap, which he pulled down firmly so that it shielded his eyes. I had laughed when he told me he had just registered for the course, partly at the chaos of the system, but also at the cheerful way in which he announced his arrival. He had then made excuses about not handing in an assignment, and I assumed he would disappear just as suddenly.

When we reached a roundabout ahead of Qalandia checkpoint, there were soldiers in riot gear marching across it. A lot of cars were avoiding Qalandia, taking a circuitous route through the nearby refugee camp. Qalandia is the main access point between the northern West Bank and Jerusalem. It was often busy with people going in and out of Israel to work, and it had also become a flashpoint for protests. Our vehicle ploughed on. There was smoke everywhere. There was a fire by the checkpoint, and dozens of young boys and teenagers were gathered there. As we got closer, I saw a group of adults—including two Westerners—run towards us, on my side of the *servees*, holding their mouths. The driver called something over his shoulder and everyone closed the windows.

There were queues of traffic moving in the opposite direction at Qalandia, and Qais said that it amazed him that everyone carried on driving past. He said that our *servees* was relatively new, so it could keep the tear gas out. 'Every time it's like that, I just hope I won't get shot,' he said.

'How do you like Ramallah?' he asked me after we had got off the *servees* and were walking through town.

I said that I liked it a lot.

'I don't understand. Some English people seem to prefer it to home.'

Without knowing I would, I said that I liked the sense of community there was in Ramallah and talked about the gap between rich and poor in the UK. Qais asked me if this inequality dated back to Mrs. Thatcher. 'I am a big fan of hers,' he said. 'Partly because everyone here—they are such leftists, into Communism or socialism.' Qais told me that he thought being on the left meant never saying anything was your fault. He had become a fan of Thatcher after watching her speeches on

YouTube.

As we were talking, Qais asked if I would mind if he stopped in a shop to buy some cheese. He scouted the shelves carefully, and explained that there had been an effort in Ramallah to stock fewer Israeli goods. 'But I don't want to buy any by accident.'

# 7

# Some boy

Ruqaya opened her bag and showed Dunia something that looked like a pencil case. Her gesture said: 'Do you think it's OK?' Dunia shrugged, as if to say 'why not?' and tilted her head towards me. We were sitting at the back of a *servees* to Ramallah. They exchanged some words in Arabic, and then Dunia turned to me: 'We decided it's OK. I said "it's only Dr. Tom."' It transpired that the small case was a make-up bag. By the time we passed through the checkpoint near Al-Ram, the two women were balancing at unlikely angles, holding a small mirror between them and applying lipstick.

Some of the students were putting on a production of Caryl Churchill's short play 'Seven Jewish Children', and I had been asked to help out with pronunciation. After the rehearsal, when we got to the playground that was used as a *servees* stop, it was crowded. A group of young men was about to push ahead of us, but Dunia and Ruqaya stood in front of the door, with their shoulders almost touching, to reserve a place. They insisted that I join them. I caught, from their attitude and stray words of Arabic, that they said to the men something like: 'He's our doctor, and he's with us.'

The two women looked almost identical at first. They were dressed in a similar way, each wearing dark jeans and a long-sleeved cotton shirt. Neither of them wore the hijab, and both had thin black hair. Dunia's hair was slightly shorter and she spoke in a louder voice, and moved her whole body as she spoke with ease and confidence. Ruqaya spoke more softly and held more of herself in reserve. When I caught the *servees* with students I was teaching, they would usually talk directly to me. But Dunia and Ruqaya talked almost as if I wasn't there. As the *servees* tilted down the hill into Abu Dis, they debated the merits of one of the other lecturers. Ruqaya liked him, but Dunia said she didn't understand what was being taught and that he could not keep control of the class.

After about ten minutes, we reached a roundabout near Ma'ale Adumim. It is one of the largest settlements in the West Bank, with a population of nearly 40,000. The word 'settlement' suggests a temporary site, which might be quickly uprooted. Yet most of the 350,000 Israeli settlers in the West Bank live in large cities.

There was a small line of men waiting for a *servees* home, each one standing apart from the others and drooping by the side of the road. One looked up hopefully as we passed and then went back to staring at the pavement. They were Palestinians who worked in Ma'ale Adumim. The *servees* picked up speed as it entered a motorway, but then we were sent shuddering forward in our seats as our driver braked. A car had pulled out in front of us and was hovering half in each lane, so we could not overtake it. When we finally passed it, I saw the driver hunched over the wheel. There were *payot* curling down his cheeks, the sidelocks that are worn by many in the Orthodox Jewish community. There were often mini-battles between Israeli and Palestinian drivers on the roads near the settlements.

Dunia and Ruqaya started to talk about exchange trips they had been on. Dunia had been to England and Belgium, and Ruqaya had been to Greece. My students could be wry about the fact that they only got to leave the West Bank on schemes that were funded to make them talk to Israelis. They could not escape the occupation, even abroad. Ruqaya told me about her trip to Greece: 'When we got into town on the last night, we had our photo taken with the waiter because we had not seen a boy all week.' Dunia had recently visited London. 'I couldn't believe it. There was this street where everyone spoke Arabic! This boy passed me and said *hillwe*. He thought I was cute! *Hillwe*. I couldn't believe it.' I asked her what she thought of England. 'I realised if you say "in a minute" in English—well, an English minute is about two hours in Palestine.' Dunia had a Jordanian passport as well as a Jerusalem ID. She talked about making trips to Tel Aviv recently and said that she preferred the shops there to the ones in Ramallah.

The *servees* reached a steep road by a quarry and joined a queue behind a lorry that was inching its way up the hill. There were half-a-dozen cars in front of us and, every now and then, one would poke its shoulder out into the left-hand lane, looking for an opening in the oncoming traffic. But there was a steady blur of cars passing us in the other direction. We trundled slowly past a clutch of Bedouin shacks with corrugated iron roofs. A woman was gathering together clothes that were hanging on a line. A small boy sat on a donkey on the hill behind her.

When we passed the small checkpoint, the two women put the make-up away. We could see black smoke billowing in the near-distance. 'Qalandia exploded,' Dunia said. When we reached it, there were dense queues of traffic. In the distance, by the Wall, I could see three or four boys moving stealthily along, hiding behind what seemed like the broken top of a table or part of a door. As we slowed on the road, boys—pre- and early-teens—were moving in and out of the traffic jam, with rocks in their hands. One was showing a small length of wood to a friend. They had scarves around the bottom of their faces, with only their eyes showing and these were lit with an expression I recognised in boys that age, mischievous and excited.

Tear gas exploded to our left. I couldn't see soldiers, but we heard a gunshot as we passed. 'They're hiding,' Ruqaya said. Dunia said she did not understand why the boys went to the Wall to throw stones.

As we picked up speed, on the way into Ramallah, Ruqaya said she wanted there to be another uprising. Dunia recalled that during the second intifada, the uprising in the early 2000s, school had been disrupted. 'My mother is a teacher, so we had school at home.' She said that everyone's grades had dropped that year, and that her sister's husband had lost two brothers. The women asked for my opinion, and I said that I thought they shouldn't have to choose between two bad options, a violent response or accepting the situation. But Ruqaya was insistent: 'It's better to do something than nothing,' she said, 'At least then the men can be martyrs and go to heaven. We have to defend our land.' Dunia's face tightened with emotion. 'Getting the *servees* across the West Bank is defending it,' she said.

* * *

Noor told me that they had a phrase in Arabic that applied to Mercutio. 'It's pronounced *mota rakhesa*,' she explained, as she wrote it out for me. 'It means that he had a cheap death.' I had set an oral exam for the Shakespeare class, in which they had to memorise one speech from *Romeo and Juliet*. I wanted to make use of the students' ability to memorise texts and for them to get to know one of the characters a little better. Noor had chosen Mercutio's speech about Queen Mab's effect on lovers: 'she gallops night by night / Through lovers' brains, and then they dream of love.' Others opted for the Prince interrupting a street fight in the first scene or the Nurse's speech about weaning Juliet as a baby.

I put a sign-up sheet for the oral exam on the door to the office, and I discovered that forty students were registered for the Shakespeare course. There were several names that were new to me. On average, there had only been about thirty students at the seminars. Not all of the students appeared for the exam, and a small number turned up and asked for extra time, one of whom elaborately described a sore tooth that was troubling him.

It was the first time that I interacted with all the students one to one. Tamam told me that, as he was the Prince, I had to imagine him arriving on a horse. One of the women, Ameera, was so nervous that she breathed heavily and kept up a dialogue with herself in Arabic. She told me she had chosen the Prince's speech because her name meant 'princess.' Adel explained that he thought Mercutio was a 'real man' who is against love, whereas Romeo follows his emotions. Two of the women, Inas and Anan, had stayed up all night practicing the Nurse's speech together. They had brought props: an apron which each of them tied around their waist and a towel, which they folded and re-folded as they spoke. They were mimicking a version they had seen online, and each of them stared past me at a memory of the baby Juliet, conjured in the mid-distance. 'I don't think I will ever forget this speech,' Inas said.

In the afternoon, a woman called Zahrah came in, dressed in tight jeans and a small t-shirt. She made a reasonable job of the speech, but most of her preparation seemed to be in urging me to give her a good mark, through solicitous smiles and gestures. After her, a man called Abd came in. He had a shaved head and was well-built. Abd stumbled through his speech and seemed close to tears. 'Are you OK?' I asked, finally realising the tears were not just a sign of nerves. He said that he had been engaged to Zahrah but that she had recently broken it off. 'How did she do in her exam?' he asked.

\* \* \*

'So who read the story?' I asked. The students were starting to be more open with me, even when they had not done the reading. A few of them said they had been too busy, because they'd had exams; one man said he had been ill. A couple of others volunteered that they had read the story, Kipling's 'Lispeth', but found the language difficult.

'I read the title,' Haytham said.

'And?'

'I thought I wouldn't like it.'

Marah said she'd read the story on the *servees*, to distract herself because the driver was going too quickly.

Kipling's story is set in India during British rule. Lispeth, who is Indian, lives with an English chaplain after her parents die. One day she returns home carrying an Englishman, whom she has found unconscious and who she plans to marry. The man is persuaded by the chaplain's wife to play along, on the grounds that Lispeth will forget him when he leaves. However, when the man fails to return and Lispeth finds out about the lie, she is appalled and 'reverts to her own people.'

Lispeth walks for twenty or thirty miles every day, while the English ladies walk for a mile or so. I told the students about Fadi's phrase that English people 'don't know how to walk.' I gave the students an extract from a letter that Kipling wrote in 1895, in response to a request for a reference from the Board of Foreign Missionaries:

> It seems to me cruel that white men, whose governments are armed with the most murderous weapons known to science, should amaze and confound their fellow creatures with a doctrine of salvation imperfectly understood by themselves and a code of ethics foreign to the climate and instincts of those races whose most cherished customs they outrage and whose gods they insult.

We read a paragraph that describes Lispeth as a 'savage' and the chaplain's wife as 'a good Christian' and talked about irony. When we read the end of the story, the students noted that Lispeth seems more upset about the lie than about her lost husband. 'How can what he and you said be untrue?' she asks the chaplain's wife, who replies: 'We said it as an excuse to keep you quiet, child.'

\* \* \*

'Will you read the part, doctor?'

Only a few students had shown up to the rehearsal, so Dunia asked me to read the second conversation, which is set in the aftermath of the Second World War and which includes this section:

Tell her this is a photograph of her grandmother, her uncles
   and me
Tell her her uncles died
Don't tell her they were killed
Tell her they were killed
Don't frighten her.

In each scene in 'Seven Jewish Children', a group of adults debates what a child should be told about an event that is unfolding, from the Nazi Holocaust to the 2008 bombing of Gaza. Most of the lines begin 'Tell her' or 'Don't tell her.'

There was a debate among the students about how many speakers the lines I had read should be divided between and whether the photograph would be projected on a screen behind the actors, so that the audience could see it. Ruqaya suggested that the students should write an additional scene, set in Gaza or the West Bank, which they could add on to the end of the play. 'I want to show that we tell the truth to our children,' she said. 'We don't *lie*.' I was going to ask why someone might soften the truth for a child. But I could not find the right words and the moment passed.

Churchill's play was controversial when it was first performed. The lawyer Anthony Julius's reading of it is similar to Ruqaya's. He sees it as part of a revival of anti-Semitism in England, and he characterises the message of the play as: 'These Jews are liars. They abuse their own children by lying to them, in order to conceal their greater, more lethal abuse of Palestinian children.' I had not read the play before, but I thought there was more to it than that.

The dilemma that is faced by the adults in the second conversation was a real one for my grandparents. Tibor and Lisl were able to leave Vienna in 1938 because Tibor had worked for a British firm and obtained a work permit to come to London. But Lisl's mother, father and stepparents all died in concentration camps, along with many of their other relatives and friends. My father, growing up in the 1950s, knew that the Germans had killed members of his family, but it was rarely spoken about. There are accounts of a similar reluctance to talk about the Holocaust in other families. After the war, many survivors were traumatised by their experiences and some felt shame that the Jewish community had 'allowed' these events to happen. There was also no larger narrative: 'the Holocaust' only emerged as a recognised description in the 1960s (and today many in the Jewish community still use the biblical term *shoah*, meaning 'the calamity').

The philosopher Stanley Cavell has written about the difficulty of knowing, with any certainty, that I am in pain or that you are. He suggests that *knowing* someone is in pain is not a matter of certainty, but of sympathy:

> But why is sympathy expressed in this way? Because your suffering makes a *claim* upon me. It is not enough that I *know* (am certain) that you suffer—I must do or reveal something (whatever can be done). In a word, I must *acknowledge* it, otherwise I do not know what "(you or his) being in pain" means.

Sometimes 'don't tell her' is an attempt to shield either a child (or the speaking adult) from pain. At such times, it signals a limit in what it is possible to say. The adults in 'Seven Jewish Children' are not lying. They are trying to find words to acknowledge what has happened: 'tell her this'; 'no, that's not quite right, tell her this'; 'don't tell her *that*....' How *could* one tell a child about events of this kind?

I had been warned that it would be a bad idea to tell my students that I was Jewish. I had spoken to Khalid about it when we met up in the UK and he had said that most people at Al-Quds would not mind. But he advised me to wait until I knew people before telling them; he thought that a few students might react badly. I do not routinely identify as Jewish in England—my mother is Christian, and Jewish identity is often seen as passing through the maternal line—so it did not feel like a deception. In fact, I thought that telling my students I was Jewish might be more of an act than concealing the fact. But when I read the scene from 'Seven Jewish Children', I came uncomfortably close to speaking about my own family history, without acknowledging the connection.

Here is another extract from my father's interview with Lisl:

David: So were you very aware of being Jewish, even at quite a young age?

Lisl: Yes, one couldn't help that in Vienna. Our neighbour, next door, in the Nedergasse—the father was an architect, so they were educated people—and the boy, who was a year or two younger, ran after me in the street and shouted 'Jewish girl,' but meant as an insult. He still lives there I hear. (D: The boy?) The boy! It's a funny thought, he's eighty too probably—some boy! [Laughs]

D: So what did you feel about being Jewish at that time?

L: I didn't have any special feelings. This sort of minor incident was....

D: Was it something your family talked much about?

L: My grandfather still was keeping... I mean they didn't keep kosher but he had a Seder there and on Friday evenings we always had a meal with the grandparents, a special one, with candles. He must have gone to synagogue too, but of that I'm not sure.

D: So you never went to synagogue?

L: No.

Lisl's experiences were not unusual. Many of those who were killed by the Nazis had been secular or did not think of themselves as Jewish. Yet being Jewish was of crucial importance to Lisl. My father has told me that he found himself reluctant to tell people that he was Jewish until well into his fifties. It may be that he (and I) had learnt unconsciously that it could be a dangerous thing to reveal.

I did not know how my students might react, but I knew that it would change my relationship to them if I announced that my father was Jewish. I thought it would mean making a claim on them—asking them to acknowledge my family's history, for example—before I had understood or acknowledged their situation, before I knew them. Given that I was in a position of relative power (not only as their teacher), I did not think I had a claim on their sympathies. I also could not connect Israel's behaviour with the Jewish traditions I knew well, which emphasise social justice and doing whatever one can to alleviate the suffering of others. There were uncomfortable parallels, for example, between Lisl's experiences and the stories that my Palestinian friends shared with me. Several told me where their grandparents had lived before 1948; they recalled old neighbours and they could name the Israeli families who had moved into their former homes.

The final conversation in Churchill's play is set during Operation Cast Lead, Israel's assault on Gaza in 2008.

Tell her the Hamas fighters have been killed
Tell her they're terrorists
Tell her they're filth

Don't
Don't tell her about the family of dead girls
Tell her you can't believe what you see on television
Tell her we killed the babies by mistake

Here the situation is almost too much for one of the speakers ('Don't'). These parents are not lying. But they are refusing to acknowledge their own pain about what is happening ('Don't') or the suffering of others: 'you can't believe what you see on television.' The humanity of the Palestinians is dissolved in a series of insults: 'Tell her they're terrorists / Tell her they're filth.' I can see why this scene might seem exaggerated.

While I was writing this book, in the summer of 2014, Israel again launched an assault on Gaza. The UN estimated that 2,104 Palestinians died, including 495 children. I got into an altercation on Facebook with an old school friend, who was defending Israel's actions and who blamed the Palestinians for putting all of their money into funding terrorism. 'There is no peace process on earth that would satisfy these extremists,' he wrote.

It was starting to grow dark when we reached Ramallah after the rehearsal. I walked with Omar, one of the other actors, while Dunia and Ruqaya chatted behind us. Omar was tall and handsome, and he was at ease with himself in a way that was unusual among the men I taught, many of whom were restless. Omar asked me if Dunia had been talking about Tel Aviv again, and said that her attitude towards going there was a kind of innocence. He told me that he was engaged but that he had a West Bank ID and his fiancée had a Jerusalem one, which meant he could not move to live with her or build a house there. 'I know where my family home was,' he said, giving the name of a town in Israel. 'But I was born in Hebron and I live in Ramallah. These are my homes now. Israelis my age were born there, it's their home. It's not that we want them to leave,' he said. 'We just want to live.'

# 8

# When I was out

After the fight on the afternoon we finished reading *Romeo and Juliet*, the university was closed for a few days. Then payday came and went, without our salaries arriving, and the union called a strike. Almost all of the staff belonged to the union, so the university closed. I knew that Lynn was struggling, and I heard that students had collected money and taken it to her house. When I texted her, she replied: 'I'll be ok, I think, for a bit. My landlord let the rent slide and gave me 800 shekels because he knew I was flat broke. Somehow the people here find a way.'

A couple of days into the strike, Basilah, one of the lecturers in the English Department, posted a picture of a student called Yousuf on Facebook. I remembered him from the exam I had invigilated in January. He had been making jokes to catch my attention. In the other pictures I had seen of him on the students' Facebook group, he was always smiling. He had a small neat mouth and both his half-grown moustache and his thick eyebrows were often arched, as if his whole face was smirking. But in Basilah's picture, his face was marked with bruises and he was looking away from the camera. Basilah wrote that Yousuf had come to see her a week before, to explain why he had missed an exam. He lived in Anata refugee camp. He and some friends had been throwing stones at soldiers, because a camp resident had been seized that morning. Yousuf had been caught and beaten by the soldiers.

The story was brutal, but it had a further twist. Yousuf had an American passport, which had expired in 2009 and no other citizenship papers. When he showed the soldiers his passport, he was taken to a hospital in Jerusalem for treatment. The irony was that Yousuf was normally unable to enter the city, even though his parents both had Jerusalem IDs; Israel refused to confer that identity on Yousuf and his siblings. Basilah had asked him why he did not renew his American passport. 'Because then they'll deport me,' he said.

\* \* \*

Ahmed drove us out into the fields beyond the village to buy milk for his mother. He stopped the car by the road, and we walked up a track towards a shack, built out of tarpaulin, torn bits of wood, and corrugated iron. There were two mattresses on the roof, held in place by rocks. Inside, there was a large brown-and-white cow, and a man was milking her. To his left, propped up on a couple of old car tyres, was a piece of wood with a few Hebrew letters on it. The man had a neat white beard and a gentle smile. As we tiptoed around his land, it felt like we were poking about inside his house. 'He sleeps out here,' Ahmed said. Ahmed gestured for me to follow him, and we peered into a shed, where there were about a dozen black, white and grey puppies, clambering over one another. There was a crate with old Coke bottles, full of milk, on the back of a truck.

We had spent the day with Ahmed's family. After we had collected the milk, we drove up to a hill above the village. 'If anyone waves to you,' Ahmed said in the car, 'wave back, or they'll think you're arrogant.' As we drove slowly through the centre of Ni'lin, each of the men we passed on the street raised his hand or smiled. Ahmed laughed: 'You might as well just keep your hand in the air.' He told me that there are around 6,000 people in Ni'lin, but only about six families.

From the hill, we could see Ni'lin to the right below us, spread out in circles around the minaret at the centre of town. The village gradually folded out into farmland and its borders were marked loosely by a series of hills which were disappearing in the dusk. To the left we could see Israel. In the middle-distance, there was a settlement, recognisable from its mixture of chalk-white houses and a few high-rise buildings. In the foreground there was a cluster of houses with red roofs, a more recent settlement, which plunged down in a V-shape towards Ni'lin, like the tip of a landslide that had stopped just short of the village.

When we had arrived in the morning, Ahmed's father had spoken to me in Hebrew and Ahmed explained that he assumed any visitors were Israeli. Now, as we drove down the hill, Ahmed pointed out Hebrew text on some of the shops. He said that settlers came into the village, especially on the Jewish Sabbath, because goods were cheaper than in the settlements. Ni'lin is next to the Wall, and there had been protests every Friday as it was built. Some estimates suggested that the village had lost up to 30% of its land.

While I had been hanging out with Ahmed, his wife Sana and their children had spent their time with Ahmed's mother and his sisters. We reunited for the journey home. About halfway back to Ramallah, which is a forty-minute drive from Ni'lin, we stopped and walked into a small field set back from the road. Ahmed had been talking throughout the day about where he might buy land to build a house. He wanted enough space that his sons could build there too. As we stood in the vacant plot, Ahmed and his wife, Sana, circled one another, while their sons ran about. Sana cupped her pregnant belly. They both smiled but did not speak. As we got back into the car, Ahmed said that he wanted to buy in Ni'lin and he was quiet for a few minutes. 'But I would have to stay in Abu Dis during the week, and return home at weekends.' He explained that there was a highway intersecting the West Bank, which could get him to campus more quickly, but that only Israelis were permitted to use it.

The *servees* journey from Ramallah to Nablus, which I visited a few days after we went to Ni'lin, had none of the manic intensity of the ride to Abu Dis. The road was mostly through hills, but at one point the land to the right flattened out and there were farmers scattered across it. The fields were divided between strips that were a deep green and those where people were working, which were a rich brown, the colour of earth newly exposed to the sun.

Nablus felt more like a city, whereas Ramallah was an overgrown town. The city centre was flat but it was overlooked by houses perched on all sides. There was a central street full of shops selling toys, shoes and electrical items. There was also a banal shopping mall and a cinema, which was showing the new James Bond film. Behind the main street was the old city, which was full of fruit sellers, herb shops, and narrow alleyways. As I tried to get my bearings, the sun passed a high building to my left. It lit an open-fronted shop, where a man was beating the sole of a shoe. Two women sat waiting, illuminated in profile, on either side of him.

Naseer Arafat, an architect, has commented:

> I would say that Nablus, at the time that it was built as an Islamic city, during the Mamluk Ottoman period, it was the center of everything. It was the capital of trade [...] In modern history, before the Israeli occupation, there were four buses leaving Nablus every morning—one to Beirut, one to Damascus, one to Jerusalem, and one to Amman. Every morning. My father used to say he would arrive in Damascus before shops opened.

As the *servees* was leaving the city, we moved slowly through traffic. At one point, we stopped beside a bus stop, where a small crowd of Israeli teenagers was waiting. Their shirts hung over their trousers and one young man had a guitar slung over his shoulder.

\* \* \*

I had started reading some poems by Walid Khazendar, in translations by the Northern Irish poet, Tom Paulin. The first stanza of one poem, 'Belongings', reads:

Who entered my room when I was out
and moved the vase on the mantelpiece just a tad?
who skewed that print—a Crusader—on the far wall?
and those pages loose on my desk
they're a shade dishevelled aren't they?

I put the poem up on the Facebook group, and asked the students what they made of it. One student said she thought it was about someone who had been away from home for a long time, who did not recognise his surroundings; another that it was about an intruder; someone else that it was about a forgetful person. I explained the ambiguity in the title—that it might mean possessions or 'belonging' to a place—and somebody said it was 'definitely a Palestinian poem.' It captured the mixture of paranoia and suspicion that one often felt in the West Bank.

A week into the strike, Ahmed wrote to Lynn and me: 'The union says that the university hasn't tried even to negotiate or to offer whatever money it has. No one knows when and how much we will get paid. The situation is very bad, and I am afraid it will get worse.' The university was dependent on student fees, which had been slow to arrive because so many families were short of money. There were rumours that if the university gave up its campus in Jerusalem and its name, it would get more funding from the Israeli Council for Higher Education. It could thus become one of the 'foreign' universities in the West Bank. For now, we were told that a senior administrator had been dispatched to one of the Gulf countries in search of short-term funds.

Ahmed said that he blamed the occupation for the university's plight but also the surrounding Arab countries for their indifference. 'They want to choke us to death and close the university.' Lynn wrote back: 'Who is "they"? I don't know who is who anymore, who is a friend and who is an enemy.'

A few days later, there was a debate on the Facebook group, started by a boy called Sami, who seemed to be friends with Qais and Haytham. Sami put up a post suggesting that 'if Edward Said was a Muslim he would have never achieved what he had achieved regarding Orientalism.' His point seemed to be that although many Muslims were capable of the kind of thinking that Said exemplified, most 'aren't capable and sometimes not willing to liberate their thoughts from the life-long teachings that made them only act as a mirror of the Western projection of thoughts about the orient.' He credited various shifts in his own perspectives to the American and American-educated teachers he'd had. One of those tutors, a Palestinian-American who had now returned to Detroit, was one of the first to reply:

> On Edward W. Said, let me say that he broke new ground. However, let's not idealize too much. He had his own blind- nesses and limitations. He is mostly a product of the West, regardless of how much he emotionally affiliated with 'Palestine,' and while he defended Palestine and also Islam, he fell into some thought traps.... Your 'American' teachers may have provided you with a more open thought perspective, but how much did they analyze or make you analyze their own system? Let's not go from an extreme of fundamentalist freezing of thought to the self-colonizing admiration of the West. It's the West that has caused many of our difficulties today, as it still does. We should liberate our minds on our own and produce our own system.

There were various replies. I said that I wondered whether there was a general issue about letting go of assumptions. Sami replied:

> I agree that everyone faces difficulties in letting go of assump- tions and even knowing they were assumptions but the reason I was very specific and mentioned the Islamic- mentality as an example is because I've been following news about the Muslim Brotherhood and the 'Salafi' Egyptians and

in most of the debates nothing they say or stand up for seems of this age but rather 300 or 400 years old. They hold debates with secular scholars or renovating Muslim researchers but not in any of the debates they accepted or agreed to any point that goes against their views. That was a case of fundamentalists, I want to also point to the case of normal people which I'm more interested in. Students of our department rarely receive the analysis tools needed for spotting an assumption and studying it unless they take courses with professors who studied abroad and I'm not saying this because of my admiration of America (I love Hollywood though!) but because I admire the quality of education there nothing more. Not idealizing them at all! I chose to refer to the US because of my American tutors as you helped me go through the journey of discovering self-colonizing things within me. If it weren't for you, God knows which branch of the Palestinian security forces I'd be working for as a blindfolded soldier following orders from uneducated officers!

I was struck by the complexity of the debates the students were having on Facebook. I also knew that, although Sami was praising his teachers from abroad, I lacked the local insights that his Palestinian-American tutor had drawn on.

It often took me a while to work out who students were on Facebook, as they sometimes used a pseudonym or a variation of their name. And whereas the men posted frequent photographs of themselves, posing singly or with one another, the women used generic images—usually of flowers, or a fashion shoot—as their profile picture.

A student called Ameera, who I did not know, posted a link to an article in the *Daily Mail*:

Dozens of Palestinians protesting against British policy have tried to attack a senior British diplomat while on a visit to a university today. The hostile demonstration forced the British consul general, Sir Vincent Fean, to cancel a speech at the Birzeit University near Ramallah. He was not hurt, although one demonstrator was seen kicking him in the shins. Student activists said they were protesting against decades of British policy supporting Israel over Palestinians.

Haytham was the first to post a comment:

I've been arguing this point with lots of my friends because they're seeing what Birzeit students have done [as] heroic, I'm pretty much sad because of what they did because this is not the right way to deal with things even though the British government were the main reason we're occupied, things will never be solved this way. We better learn how to deal with things in a civilized way.

Ameera had challenged him, saying she saw little that was 'uncivilised' about the protest: 'I'd rather hear honest, open and totally justified anger being expressed than mealy-mouthed diplomatic speeches. We've had enough of the latter.' Haytham suggested that it might have been better to debate with the diplomat openly ('and he would start blushing on TV'), but Ameera was unconvinced. Haytham concluded:

Then according to what you're suggesting this is the best way things will get accomplished and this is the exact way our voices are going to be heard! Ain't that what they need in order for them to complete their theory that we Palestinians are terrorists?!

\* \* \*

When I went to Tel Aviv, to get a visa from the Jordanian

embassy, it was my first time outside the West Bank since I had arrived, and the journey was disarmingly quick. It was a hot day and, within a few hours of leaving Ramallah, I was sitting on a crowded beach in Tel Aviv. It was about 4pm and the sea was full of people. I went for a pizza, and then I spent an aimless evening watching football. Lionel Messi scored two goals for Barcelona, and I knew that the coffee shops in Ramallah would be full of people watching the game. Everyone in the West Bank followed the Spanish league, which was broadcast on Al-Jazeera. I got a little drunk, which was lucky, as when I got back to the hotel, there was loud music seeping into my room from a nearby club.

On the way to Tel Aviv, I had stopped in Jerusalem. I poked my head into the post office, hoping to find a passport photo machine, and a security guard directed me to a shop around the corner. The woman spoke little English. She gestured for me to sit on a stool, with a deep sigh, then lined up the camera. She started to tut and walked away, returning with a clutch of tissues and pointing to my sweaty forehead. I wiped my brow and she went on with the photographs. As I was paying, I asked her where I could find the *sheroot* stop. The *sheroot* is the Israeli equivalent of the *servees* and it was a quick and cheap way of travelling between cities. The woman sighed, rolled her eyes and made a vague gesture with her hand. I wasn't sure if she was pointing the way I should go, or dispensing with me.

While I was waiting for the visa, I walked a mile or so to the Tel Aviv Museum of Art. I skimmed through a room full of early twentieth-century European artists like Picasso and Braque, which would normally have absorbed me. In the basement, there was an installation by Douglas Gordon. Two enormous screens were set at right angles to one another. They depicted two Israeli musicians of Polish descent, who were filmed travelling to Poland and then performing there. The film was about fifty minutes long, on a loop. They were performing Mozart's Sinfonia Concertante in E Flat Major K.364. The camera angles caught the

two players, in different kinds of intensity. One had a shaggy
fringe; the other was bald. They both smiled occasionally, with
satisfaction, and glanced at one another to judge timing or
phrasing. When the film looped back to the start, I found that I
couldn't stay with it. I wandered out of the gallery, and back into
the street. I kept thinking that the installation had a 'palpable
design upon us,' as Keats said of poetry of a similar kind. It felt
like the story was being used as propaganda. But I knew too that
my own sense of alienation was putting everything I encountered at a distance.

I had started to find it difficult to leave the West Bank. When
I left for good, at the end of May, it was a painful experience. I
know this is a common occurrence for expats, what one might
call the difficulties of re-entry. But there is also a particular
intensity to life in Palestine. The 'situation,' as it is called,
becomes all-pervasive. When I met friends in Ramallah, we often
started by exchanging the latest news: 'Have you heard about
what happened at Qalandia?', 'There's a rumour that a prisoner
died', 'Did you hear about the teacher who was refused entry?'
The situation binds itself into one's day-to-day experience. For
several months after I came home, I found myself either inserting
anecdotes from my time in the West Bank into any space I could
find in a conversation or feeling it hover out of reach as though
it was too large an experience to integrate into my reality at
'home'. (I also saw my university in England from a disconcerting new angle. Just after I got home, there was a strike about
pay, which only a smattering of staff observed. 'You call this a
strike?' I wanted to ask.)

I could still see that there were different perspectives within
Israel/Palestine. But while I was living in the West Bank it felt
like I wasn't crossing a border if I travelled into Jerusalem, but
moving from one country's unconscious into its ego—moving
between two parts of a whole that lived in constant tension with
one another. Whereas in the West Bank, the occupation

permeates everything, in Israel what was striking was the denial about what was happening just a few miles away. At around the time I went to Tel Aviv, Lily, one of my friends in Ramallah, had some friends from England staying with her. She had taken them on various trips across the West Bank, and one of the girls said just before she left: 'I just feel like I need to see the other side now.' Lily had lost it, half to her own surprise. 'This isn't a war,' she shouted. 'There *isn't* another side.'

\* \* \*

I left my suitcase in the cupboard, and packed a large sports bag with as many clothes as I could carry. I pushed some suntan lotion I had not used into one of the side pockets, alongside my Kindle and a few books. I left my laptop behind, because it now had Arabic letters superimposed on the keyboard, and I tidied all of my teaching materials away in a cupboard.

As a visiting academic in the West Bank, it is difficult to obtain a working visa. I had arrived on a tourist visa and I had to leave the country after three months in order to renew it. I had decided to go to Jordan for a few days. So I packed a bag that could have belonged to someone who had been travelling around Israel for a few months. I knew it was possible I would be refused entry or given a week's visa on my return, just long enough to get my stuff.

On the way back from Jordan, I travelled via Eilat—a tourist resort at the very southern tip of Israel—and then I started the long journey by bus back up the east coast to Jerusalem. It was hot in Eilat, and the bus station was cramped, with people sprawled in every corner of the small building. When I got on to the bus, it was nearly full and the only spare seat was next to mine. Soon after we set out, a young woman in her 20s, with bleached-blonde hair and a wild look in her eye, stood by my seat and started shouting at me in Hebrew, claiming that I was in her seat. She had a tired and jaded look. She also spoke to two women in front of me, who had curly black hair and who looked as if they were sisters. One of the women, who was agitated, eventually went and sat at the front. The blonde woman came back and shouted at me again, and I eventually worked out that she wanted my seat and the one next to it because she and her son were separated.

The journey takes about ten hours and, halfway through, the bus stops at a service station. I went to buy some food, and when I came back to the coach the two women who had been in front of me were sitting on the curb. One of them sat shyly to the side and did not make eye contact, but the other looked up at me under her fringe.

'I'm sorry about the crazy woman,' she said. She asked me what I was doing in Israel and I said that I was a tourist.

I asked her where she was from.

'We're from Jerusalem.'

There was a pause, and we caught one another's eye.

'We are Palestinians,' she said.

'I live in Ramallah,' I replied. Her name was Dalia and she explained that she did not understand Hebrew. 'I wanted to help you,' she said. About five minutes before the bus was due to leave, its engine suddenly revved on. 'They can be quite impatient,' Dalia said.

As the bus made its way along the coast of the Dead Sea, I found myself daydreaming about being back in Ramallah, even about staying there for good. When we got near Jerusalem, I darted off the bus, relieved to be nearly home, and started looking around for a taxi. I saw that Dalia and her sister had got off too, and that they were making their way towards me. 'Our brother lives in Ramallah, he's coming to collect us. Would you like a lift?'

\* \* \*

When I got home in the evenings, I would sometimes sit in the lobby of my apartment building, chatting to a young man named Qusay, who worked for my landlord doing odd jobs. He told me he had trained as an accountant, but that he could not get a job because he did not have *'wasta'* or 'vitamin w.' He said that *'wasta'* meant having access to power or social clout; in Palestine, I was told, you needed to know someone in power in order to get on. Qusay told me that he thought everything had changed in Ramallah after Yasser Arafat had died. He said that one of his school friends was now a low-ranking Palestinian Authority employee, but he had three cars, a motorbike, and a constant stream of money. 'Before, with Arafat, people like my father felt they knew him. If they had problems, they could see him in person. But with Abbas....'

Qusay spoke an easy, colloquial English. He told me that, when he was growing up, he would speak to tourists, to learn the language. Qusay told me this account of how he learned English, several times. Then the story changed. One evening, after offering me a cigarette, he told me that he had been picked up by the intelligence service a few years before, and that they did not believe he had never been abroad, because he spoke such good English. He told me that he had been tortured and forced to sign a false confession. Qusay lamented that he was now not allowed to leave the West Bank, in spite of the fact that he had not been convicted of anything. Only slowly did I understand that it was the Palestinian security forces who had interrogated him, not the Israelis.

One evening, when I came in, Qusay started to tell me the whole story of a film he had seen, which turned out to be *Life of Pi*. He was laughing and acting it out in the lobby and he went to his room and retrieved his laptop. He skipped through a few scenes of Pi's childhood and then we watched about twenty minutes, in which the ship Pi is travelling on is destroyed in a storm. We were standing in parallel, leaning in to the screen which he had placed on the reception desk in the foyer. Qusay told me again that he could not leave the country and said that he was looking for a lawyer. Pi, meanwhile, was clambering on to a small lifeboat, which was also boarded by a zebra, a wolf and a tiger, all survivors from the wrecked ship. I asked Qusay where he would like to go. 'I want to see the world,' he said.

# 9

# You may kill me

I asked Qais to repeat his question, so the others could hear it. We had just finished reading the assassination of Julius Caesar and the confusion that follows it, during which the conspirators bathe themselves in Caesar's blood. At the start of the class, I had assigned the ten or so speaking parts. Then I told all 35 students to stand up and push the tables back. There was a pause. 'We're going to do some acting,' I said.

The scene begins with a crowd pressing in on Caesar, before he enters the Capitol. I got the actors who were reading Artemidorus and the Soothsayer, who both petition Caesar, to stand on one side of the classroom amid a group, while the rest of the students made up a crowd on the other side. We read through the dialogue, acting it out as a street scene, with individuals emerging out of the crowd, to speak to Caesar. As the students positioned themselves, it became clear that the conspirators, who are poised to kill Caesar, stand nearest to him. 'Where are the guards?' Qais asked.

As Caesar enters the Capitol, the crowd is left outside and I told most of the students to sit down. Once the senators and other notables are inside, Metellus asks 'for the repealing of my banished brother' and others echo his plea. Caesar refuses, saying: 'I am as constant as the northern star.' The students were still working out the meaning, so I mimed that they should each kneel before Caesar as they spoke. We started to form a circle around him. 'Doth not Brutus bootless kneel?' Caesar asks. The woman who was reading Brutus's part stood in front of Caesar. We debated whether Brutus would play a part in the assassination or whether he looks on cold-eyed.

Afterwards, Tamam, with a mischievous lilt to his voice,

asked: 'Is he really dead?'

'Yes,' I said.

'But is he *really* dead?'

'He's really, definitely dead.'

'We burned our books!' Tariq was smiling. 'That's it, Al-Quds University is closed for good.' It was our first class back after the strike, and I had asked the students why they hadn't read the story for that class, a Sherlock Holmes mystery called 'The Adventure of the Speckled Band'. I ended up acting it out. The story is about Helen Stoner, a 32-year-old woman who is about to marry. Her stepfather insists that she sleep in the room where her twin sister, Julia, died two years earlier. Julia's dying words were: 'The band! The speckled band!' I paused, just before I got to the end, to see if anyone could guess how the mystery was resolved. 'We have a detective in the class,' one woman said, when I gave Holmes's explanation. She told me that her friend had solved it, but that she had been too shy to say.

I had got to the *servees* stop in Ramallah at 7am that morning, expecting to miss the rush hour. But there were hardly any vehicles travelling to Abu Dis and a large crowd quickly developed. The atmosphere was frenzied and chaotic, with groups of students trying to mob each *servees* as it arrived. It was as if some of the tension that had been bottled up during the strike had spilled over. As I edged near to one *servees*, the driver said he could only take one more person. Angham, one of my students, was standing just in front of me. She pulled her friend out of the way and insisted that I take the space. I was too relieved to refuse, and I managed to say a garbled thank-you in Arabic.

We started reading *Julius Caesar* that morning and the play seemed more difficult at first: the language more dense, and the situation less accessible than in *Romeo and Juliet*. But it was also as if we were missing our familiarity with the other play. I started by asking the students about some new Arabic words I had learned. One was '*wasta*.' I asked the students why there was no directly equivalent word in English. 'Because our language is richer,' one student said, smiling. The other word I asked them about was '*fasaad*,' meaning corruption.

We talked about some of the conventions governing Rome at the time of Caesar's rule. Shakespeare's play opens with Caesar in full pomp. One of the debates in the play is about the power he has accumulated as an individual, threatening the democratic institutions on which Rome had previously relied. A conspiracy develops against him, led by Brutus, who is goaded on by Cassius. Caesar is assassinated in Act III and the rest of the play chronicles the downfall of the conspiracy. Mark Antony's famous speech at Caesar's funeral turns the crowd against the conspirators, although his deft oratory makes him appear to be supporting them at first: 'Friends, Romans, countrymen, lend me your ears / I come to bury Caesar, not to praise him.'

We read an early scene, in which Cassius tries to persuade Brutus into leading the conspiracy. 'Why does Cassius not just take power himself?' Qais asked. 'He's in MI6, isn't he? He works like the intelligence services, always undermining governments to get their own person into power.' The conspirators think of themselves as heroes and, after Caesar's death, they imagine that this is how history will view them. Brutus urges the others to walk to the market-place, with their hands stained with Caesar's blood: 'Let's all cry, "Peace, freedom and liberty!"' I pointed out that some of the historical sources that Shakespeare used were more sympathetic to Brutus and Cassius. Several students said that the evidence suggested Caesar was a good man and that the conspirators hated the common people.

I knew that Basilah read the play very differently, encouraging students to imagine it from the point of view of the conspirators, as a story about resisting tyranny. This reading has historical precedents. In 1937, Orson Welles put on a stage version subtitled 'Death of a Dictator', in which Antony's oratory—and the violent street scenes that follow it—had a new, and brutal, resonance.

At the time that we were reading the play, there was an emotional response in the West Bank to the death of the Venezuelan leader, Hugo Chavez. He had been an outspoken supporter of the Palestinians. An American I had met, who worked for an NGO in Ramallah, put up a heartfelt plea on Facebook:

The enemy of your enemy is not necessarily your friend. While his friend Bashar Al Assad slaughtered his people and your fellow Palestinians, Chavez expressed support for his rule. Chavez was very good to his supporters but equally bad to his opponents. To take just one example, when millions of his people signed a petition to try to end his rule, he published their names and directed his government to deny them jobs and basic services like passport renewal. I always wanted to believe that what Chavez said about helping the poor and standing up for human rights was true, but when I looked into it more deeply, though he did some very positive things for the poor, I saw that on the whole he was personally corrupt and did tremendous damage to his entire economy. I'm not disputing that he won elections. He was indeed a very special kind of despot, one who uses the system to put himself into power and then proceeds to dismantle that system.

\* \* \*

One afternoon, when I got back to Ramallah, I ran into Qais near Yasser Arafat Square. He was talking to another man, introduced to me as Sami, who I knew from their Facebook discussions. Sami was doing an MA at Birzeit and told me he had been writing an essay about Northern Ireland. We went for a coffee. The café we were in was showing music videos on a series of screens. Sami pointed out that the Egyptian channel put up subtitles in Arabic that were 'quite philosophical.' He said they had explained Gangnam Style as being a song about Korean culture.

It was a few weeks before Obama was due to visit the West Bank, and there were posters everywhere telling him not to bring his mobile phone, because you could not get 3G in the West Bank. I had been sceptical about the campaign, because it seemed to focus on a narrow example of how the occupation functioned. But Sami was more positive, saying it showed how the Palestinians were cut off from the rest of the world. There was noise from the street outside as we were talking. Sami stuck his head out of the window and reported that it was a protest at the death of a man who had been killed by a colleague in a village just outside Ramallah.

'It's full of Ramallah hipsters,' Sami said.

I asked how I could spot a hipster.

'They wear a scarf, even when it's warm, and dark glasses inside.'

Sami and Qais were the first students to ask me directly what I thought about the political situation. Sami said that he was in favour of one democratic state for Palestinians and Israelis. He said that he had met an Israeli during a summer camp in Greece, who was in the right-wing party Likud. This young man had contacted Sami subsequently, saying he wanted to start a party for Palestinians and Israelis arguing for one state.

'Is he sincere?' I asked.

* * *

The young man in the photograph stands at the window and leans out. To his left, there is a fragment of broken glass at the bottom of the window frame, which has the jagged shape of an iceberg. The man is shouting towards the crowd that has gathered beneath him. In the foreground of the picture, you can see the back of three heads, and three pairs of hands raised in the air. The man has raised his arms with his palms facing outwards. They are covered in blood. There are three other hands visible in the window frame, emerging from the room inside, but there are no other faces. One is the right hand of someone unseen, who is waving or signalling in another direction. The other two hands are close together at the top of the picture and they are also bloodied.

The photograph was taken in October 2000, in the midst of the second intifada. Two Israeli soldiers, Vadim Nurzhitz and Yossi Avrahami, had driven into Palestinian-controlled areas of the city by mistake. They were detained by Palestinian Authority police officers and then a crowd stormed the police station.

Abdel Aziz Salha, the man in the photograph, spoke to the *Electronic Intifada* in 2013: 'Earlier on that day, one Palestinian from Ramallah was murdered by Israeli settlers from a settlement neighbouring Ramallah. After they had killed him, they cut his ears and threw his body. This is the reason there were thousands of protestors across Ramallah on that day. Accidentally, we got word that there were two Israeli soldiers held in one Ramallah police station.' After the photograph was published, Salha became the most wanted man in the West Bank. He was released from prison 11 years later and went to live in Gaza.

In the two weeks before the incident in Ramallah in 2000, 85 Palestinians had been killed during unarmed protests, and five Israelis had died. But the rumour that reached the crowd that day, about the murder of a man from Ramallah, turned out to be false. According to the *Electronic Intifada*: 'A forensic investigation by Physicians for Human Rights later found that the man was most likely killed in a car accident.'

I had wondered, as I looked at the photograph, what the room was like behind Salha. It was almost as though the third pair of hands belonged to someone who was standing on the ceiling.

Slowly, I realised that these were the bloodied wrists of one of the victims, who must be hanging upside down.

\* \* \*

H.G. Wells's short story 'The Star', published in 1897, tells of a star entering the solar system and ultimately causing devastation as it passes close to Earth.

> And when next it rose over Europe everywhere were crowds of watchers on hilly slopes, on house-roofs, in open spaces, staring eastward for the rising of the great new star. It rose with a white glow in front of it, like the glare of a white fire, and those who had seen it come into existence the night before cried out at the sight of it. 'It is larger,' they cried. 'It is brighter!'

Wells's story lacks the consoling human adventure that is at the centre of many disaster movies. Instead, as one student pointed out, the star is the hero. There is a brutal sense of perspective. Earth is seen from Mars at the end, and the near-destruction of the planet is thus summed up from an external viewpoint. Yet there is also the perspective of one character, who is a mathematician: 'He looked at [the star] as one might look into the eyes of a brave enemy. "You may kill me," he said after a silence. "But I can hold you—and all the universe for that matter—in the grip of this little brain. I would not change. Even now."'

I had started to become impatient with the students who were not doing the reading. When we got to this story, I refused to do the work for them. 'What happens in the story?' I asked, to near silence. 'What happens at the start?' At the end of the class, I managed to say something, keeping my temper even, but hoping to be firm. I felt that I needed to be stricter. But I hated the thought of the students doing the reading only because I told them to do it. I said that I was not going to police them, but that it would limit the kinds of discussion we could have if they did not read. 'If you're not going to put the effort in, then I will put less effort in too. You have the right not to read, as we've talked about. But it's up to you to take responsibility for what you get out of the course now.' One student said quickly that he'd had several exams. There was an uneasy silence. I was trying to gauge how they were taking what I had said and how well I really understood their reasons for not doing the reading.

Just when I thought the discussion had fizzled out, Haytham spoke. 'I've been at the university for five years. I've never been asked to do this before—to come and have opinions, to do the reading only if I want to. It's usually just learning for the exam.'

'Is that a complaint?' I asked.

'It's just a big change.'

As I was preparing to leave, the student who had said he'd had exams rushed up with his phone held out in his hand: 'Did you see this, doctor?' He set the phone to play a video for me. It was a YouTube clip, shot in Chelyabinsk a few weeks earlier, showing a meteor shower on the horizon amid an explosion of light.

* * *

We had started reading *Julius Caesar* straight after the strike. In the first class back, I gave the students Michael Longley's poem 'Ceasefire', which was published in the *Irish Times* in 1994, shortly ahead of a ceasefire in Northern Ireland. The poem borrows from *The Iliad*, telling the story of Priam going to meet with his enemy Achilles, to ask for the body of his son, Hector, who has been killed in the war. Priam speaks in the final couplet:

I get down on my knees and do what must be done
And kiss Achilles' hand, the killer of my son.

The students did not know the term 'ceasefire,' so I explained it. We talked about the simple language ('do what must be done') and the order of events. The poem concludes with Priam on his knees, kissing Achilles' hand, but this must precede the opening, in which the two men weep together. I told the students that I had chosen the poem because they had said they found the ending of *Romeo and Juliet* difficult to imagine if the play was set in Palestine, but also because Longley turns to an old story to illustrate contemporary concerns. Perhaps, I suggested, Shakespeare had done the same in *Julius Caesar*.

Later, I posted the poem on the Facebook group, with a link to Longley reading it. Basilah pointed out that, initially, Achilles refuses to release Hector's body, and that he speaks to Priam not as an equal but as the representative of a conquering force. She asked: 'So, bottom line, the ceasefire is simply a ruse—or a magnanimous gesture on the part of the victor?' Ahmed replied: 'Widows, widowers, orphans might kiss the hands of self-appointed murderers and torturers. This can be applied to our situation. Ceasefire, here in Palestine, gives the Israelis more time to swallow whatever land is left. The maimed are made to forgive before they are ready to forgive.'

# 10

# Hamlet's dangerous state

'Would you like to join us?'

I had started to wilt in the heat. It was a hot afternoon in April, and there was a long wait for a *servees* back to Ramallah. Abd spotted me and asked if I wanted to get a ride with his friends: 'Then we are six.' I stood in one of the few sections of shade with Zahrah, who Abd had told me used to be his fiancée. Abd wandered around, trying to bargain with the drivers. Most of the *servees* were yellow, but there were also a few white ones at the edge of the yard, and eventually we got into one of those. Abd insisted that I sit in the front, next to the driver. As we edged down the hill, my seatbelt popped out of its holder.

According to a 2011 article in the Israeli newspaper, *Ha'aretz*, there are about seven or eight hundred white Ford Transits in the area around Al Eizariya, Abu Dis and Sawahera. Most are more than ten years old, and they are not insured. Palestinians in the West Bank are not allowed to drive Israeli cars without a permit, and they cannot buy used cars from Israel if they are more than four years old. The Wall has cut the towns off from the public transport in Jerusalem, prompting this black market in older vehicles.

When we reached the motorway beneath Ma'ale Adummin, there were traffic lights about fifty yards ahead of us. There were two Israeli cars queueing to the right, on a road leading from the settlement, waiting to cross the motorway in front of us and join it in the other direction. As the lights started to turn red, our driver sped up to get through, then slowed, and then sped up again. I watched the two cars to the right pulling out. We tore through the lights and skidded between the two cars, and I heard a scream. I was unsure whether it was from within the *servees* or from outside. By the time we came to a halt, I had slid down in my seat, with my feet braced against the floor, holding on to the handle above the window.

When we re-started, several people lit cigarettes and someone handed one to me. Abd lent forward in his seat and asked me if I was alright. As we approached Ramallah, the driver slowed down by the side of the road several times and called out questions to passers-by. When we pulled into the city, Zahrah and I were the last off. She said that she always got freshly-baked bread from a shop round the corner. We bought some and ate it as we walked. Zahrah said that students were not supposed to get the white *servees* and that the driver had been slowing down near Ramallah to ask if there were police, because he wasn't meant to be there. I asked if he had sped up because the cars were Israeli. She shook her head. 'He was insane,' she said.

Zahrah told me that her mother was from Iraq and that her father was from Syria. They had not been to Iraq since 2003.

'Is it very beautiful?' I asked.

'Like heaven,' she said.

At around this time, I was asked to cover some classes at Al-Quds Bard for a lecturer who had returned to the States for a few weeks. The students were reading *Hamlet*, as part of a first-year liberal arts course. I struggled with the new names and faces, and attendance was poor at the first class—the usual perils of being a supply teacher. One man, called Hamdi, spoke more confidently in the first class, with a slight Texan accent. The next day, I found myself sitting next to him at lunchtime on the *servees* from Ramallah. Hamdi explained that he was running late because his father was away and he'd been called in to speak to a teacher at his younger brother's school. He said that he was surprised at what his brother had been up to: 'I'm going to have to kick his ass.' Hamdi told me his family had lived in the US until he was 11, but their father had not wanted his daughters growing up in America. 'I'm taking beginners' Arabic here,' Hamdi explained.

'But my English vocabulary hasn't progressed at all. I mean, I talk to my friends in the States, and I don't know *shit*.' Hamdi asked me what sports I liked to watch, and told me he was a big fan of American football. 'I took a ball into school in Al-Bireh, and my friends were like: what is *that*?'

As we neared Abu Dis, Hamdi told me that, when he was at school, he used to tell his mother he was going to a friend's house to do homework, and he would go to Qalandia or to Ofer prison and throw rocks. 'Once I came face-to-face with a soldier, and I was still holding a rock. We both just stood there for about ten seconds. I guess he was shitting himself too. So I threw this rock—it just went *thud*, it hit him right in the chest. He stood there, looking at me, like he couldn't believe I threw it.' On another occasion, Hamdi had been shot by a rubber bullet. He told me he could fairly easily get a permit to go into Israel. 'But I've pretty much stopped going. I went to this mall once, and the soldiers were like, "It's closed." And I laughed: "But, look, I can see all these other folks going in." So I tried just walking past, and....' He raised his arms to mimic the soldiers raising their guns.

The dynamics in the classroom felt subtly different at Bard. The classes were smaller, normally about 15 students. Bard was the only university in the West Bank to offer scholarships to students from refugee camps. It also attracted the Palestinian elite, a number of whom were American-born and educated. The students mixed well socially and many were very bright. Yet there was a tinge of apathy in the atmosphere that felt more like teaching classes at home. For the first time, I had to send a student who was being disruptive out of the class.

In one of the *Hamlet* classes, we started with a quotation from early on in the play in which a minor character, Marcellus, says there is 'something rotten in the state of Denmark.' I asked what 'rotten' meant and the students described how bread goes rotten: that it changes in colour, texture and appearance; that it will smell and become inedible. Then we discussed the different meanings of the word 'state,' including as a condition that can change (e.g. 'Hamlet is in a bad mental state') or a country, and variants on this, including the question of whether Palestine had become a state following the declaration at the UN. We talked about what it would mean for any of these states to be rotten and the students had good answers: that a state could be rotten economically, politically, through corruption, war or civil war. One woman said there could be a difference between appearance and reality. We talked too about the fact that Hamlet embodies the kingdom, so that his 'state of mind' at the start of the play mirrors the political state's corruption.

We read most of the first scene, skipping through a couple of longer speeches. When we got to the point where Horatio and others each say the ghost of Hamlet's father is 'here' three times and then 'gone,' I drew a picture of the Globe Theatre. We discussed how it might be utilised in the scene, for example with the characters each blocking one of the three exits at the back of the stage and the ghost disappearing through the trapdoor.

I had begun to feel a little high on the energy of the class and I felt the students had started to understand some of what we were discussing. I checked the time and then asked if there were any questions. I was expecting us to wrap up at that point but, to my delight, one woman put her hand up immediately. She had not spoken before, and now she took a deep breath.

'What is your name?' she asked me.

I had started to wonder whether Marcellus was being more literal than is normally supposed: maybe it really *smells* in Denmark. One of the peculiarities of life in the West Bank is the endless piles of rubbish you encounter: at the sides of streets, in gardens, even on rooftops. A young American who worked at Bard told me that when he first arrived his Palestinian friends used to laugh at him if he put a sweet wrapper in his pocket instead of throwing it on the street. I was told there were three reasons for the accumulation of rubbish: the lack of proper funds for refuse collection from the Palestinian Authority; a culture in which people kept their own house tidy and clean but did not worry about the public space; and a general depression about the situation. Apparently, a huge effort had been made to clean up the West Bank in the 1990s, but the situation had deteriorated again. There was also a story that the Palestinians had to share rubbish dumps with the Israeli settlements, which were often full, and that the Palestinians could not afford to pay for extra space.

The West Bank had started to bleed into my reading of *Hamlet* in other ways too. I was asked to give a lecture on the play to the first-year students at Bard. I had been reading an essay by Hannah Arendt called 'Thinking and Moral Considerations' and I started to construct a reading of the play around it. Arendt claims that it is characteristic of thinking that it makes each of us two people instead of one and that it plunges us into indecision. I divided up one of *Hamlet*'s soliloquies into two parts to try and illustrate this to the students:

| | |
|---|---|
| Hamlet 1: | To be |
| Hamlet 2: | Or not to be |
| Hamlet 1: | —that is the question: |
| | Whether 'tis nobler in the mind to suffer |
| | The slings and arrows of outrageous fortune, |
| Hamlet 2: | Or to take arms against a sea of troubles |
| | And, by opposing, end them. To die, to sleep— |
| Hamlet 1: | no more— |
| Hamlet 2: | and by a sleep to say we end |
| | The heartache and the thousand natural shocks |
| | That flesh is heir to—'tis a consummation |
| | Devoutly to be wished. To die, to sleep— |
| | To sleep, perchance to dream |
| Hamlet 1: | Ay, there's the rub, |

> For in that sleep of death what dreams may come,
> When we have shuffled off this mortal coil,
>
> Hamlet 1/2: Must give us pause

Hamlet is in two minds—one urging him to continue, no matter what 'outrageous fortune' throws at him; the other urging him to 'end' his troubles in death. Yet the two minds together 'must pause' in their debate, because neither of them is dominant.

One of the central points of Arendt's essay is that, however dangerous thinking may be, it is equally dangerous *not* to think: 'By shielding people against the dangers of examination, it teaches them to hold fast to whatever the prescribed rules of conduct may be at a given time in a given society [...] In other words, they get used to never making up their minds.' I suggested to the students that in *Hamlet* we have a perfect example of this. Osric, a courtier who enters briefly at the end of the play, agrees with anything Hamlet tells him, including a series of contradictory statements about the weather:

| | |
|---|---|
| Hamlet: | Put your bonnet to his right use: 'tis for the head. |
| Osric: | I thank your lordship, it is very hot. |
| Hamlet: | No, believe me, 'tis very cold, the wind is northerly. |
| Osric: | It is indifferent cold, my lord, indeed. |
| Hamlet: | But yet, methinks, it is very sultry and hot for my complexion. |
| Osric: | Exceedingly my lord, it is very sultry... |

Osric's attitude will keep him safe in his own society, but might also lead him to follow *any* orders from his superiors, no matter how they would contradict reality. Osric is thus an example of what Arendt famously saw in the Nazi war criminal Adolf Eichmann, someone who is capable of evil because of an inability to think for themselves. In contrast, thinking can put you at odds with your society, your friends—or even with yourself. Hamlet's tragedy is not that he cannot make up his mind, as is often claimed, but that he is determined to make up his *own* mind, whatever the cost.

Just before the start of a Special Topics class at around this time, there was a sound like an ambulance siren outside. It was constant and it did not seem to move nearer or further away. Inas had arrived early and she told me that a prisoner had died. His name was Maysara Abuhamdia and he was suffering from cancer. I read later that his diagnosis had been delayed because he was given limited access to doctors in gaol. I started the class by asking the students to tell me about what had happened. There was some confusion about whether the man who had died had also been a hunger striker. Tariq explained that if a prisoner had been denied their humanity, going on hunger strike was a way of reclaiming some basic dignity, because it was the one thing left over which you had any choice: 'Only a human can refuse food, an animal would not.'

I asked the students whether they thought there would be another strike at the university, because of the death. 'Probably,' said one student. 'Hopefully,' said another. I suggested there were other ways of responding to this kind of incident, which would be less disruptive of their studies. I was imagining that we could have a teach-in, abandoning normal classes but discussing what was happening. 'But then we would accept that this is normal,' Inas said.

In that class, we were reading some of the Walid Khazendar poems, which I had posted online during the strike. I gave the students a handout which linked the use of the word 'rights' in Paulin's translations of the poems to the UN Declaration of Human Rights. 'Belongings' especially, with its opening question—'Who entered my room when I was out?'—seemed to speak to Article 12 of the Declaration: 'No-one shall be subjected to arbitrary interference with his property, family, home or correspondence, nor to attacks upon his honour or reputation.' I encouraged the students to follow the link I had given them and to read the Declaration. 'But why would I read it,' asked Tariq, 'when so many countries ignore it?'

A week or so later, I gave the students Franz Kafka's short story 'A Hunger Artist', which tells the story of a talented performer who finds that interest in his art, of starving himself, rapidly declines. At the end, the hunger artist is asked why he insisted on starving himself, long after the crowds had gone away. He replies:

> Because I couldn't find a food which tasted good to me. If I had found that, believe me, I would not have made a spectacle of myself and would have eaten to my heart's content, like you and everyone else.

The discussion was rapid and confusing, with some of the students talking so quickly that it was hard for me to grasp all of the points that they wanted to make.

Ruba was a slight young woman, with long black hair, who would tilt her head to the right as she spoke and look up from under her fringe. She could be unusually forceful. 'For our hunger strikers,' she said, 'there is a point to their actions. But for him, it is *pointless*.' Tariq said the story was 'suggestive,' and we discussed the fact that it was not written in a realistic style. Someone said that the story was about the value of human life. Haytham picked up Ruba's question: 'But what's the point of *any* of the stories we read?' At first, I thought the question was directed at me. But he and Ruba started to debate angrily with one another. Haytham insisted that the story was relevant. He was close to being unmanageable, and at one point seemed closed to tears. Then he did turn to me, and asked why I chose the stories for the course.

Several students stayed to keep the debate going at the end, and Wafa said that it would be good to have more 'real' debates, because normally people tended to make one point, either agree or disagree, and that was it. I was reminded of the limited debate we'd had around the Maupassant story earlier in the term. Yet I also felt uneasy, as though I had encouraged emotion in the class that I had not fully understood.

When I got back to the office, I ran into Wafa, Tariq, Haytham and a couple of their friends in the hallway outside. They offered me a cigarette and then carried on with a conversation they were having. It seemed to be connected to the Kafka story.

Eventually Tariq turned to me and said: 'Why did you give us that story?'

One of his friends leaned towards me. 'He thinks you just wanted them to make a point about the hunger strikers.'

I admitted that I tried to pick stories that I thought were relevant. 'But the worst kind of class would be one where I know exactly what you're going to say beforehand.'

Haytham spoke about a post that another lecturer had made on Facebook, advocating that Al-Quds should be teaching students how to resist the occupation. 'This would be just perfect for the Israelis, then they can bomb the university.' I asked whether students ever had debates about the curriculum, or the occupation, in class. They said that they could not discuss these issues in class, because some students were affiliated to different factions—such as Hamas, Fatah, or the Muslim Brotherhood— and they were afraid of spies, including Israeli ones. Tariq said that about 70% of Palestinians were not affiliated, and yet these groupings dominated.

Haytham told a story about coming back from a party in Bethlehem and being stopped by Israeli soldiers. He was sober, but his friends were drunk. 'One of my friends said that there had been drunk Israeli girls at the party, and a soldier put his gun to the boy's head and said: "Say that again." So my other friend got involved. And the two of them were taken away to *that* room and beaten up.' He and Tariq exchanged a glance.

As the conversation moved on, Tariq argued vigorously that you could not blame everything on Israel and the occupation. 'Look at what has been achieved in Israel, compared to how little we had done in the time before.' Haytham disagreed. He said several times, 'I am not living' and then he insisted to the others: 'We are not living.'

I said that I needed to go and catch the *servees* back to Ramallah and Haytham walked with me to the front gate. He was still furious with Ruba. He said other students were speaking in class only to show they were participating, and that all they wanted was to write down the answers, and that they would then get better marks than him. I thought Ruba was a strange target for his ire. They were well-matched as adversaries, and I was concerned that he did not always listen, especially to the women in the class. I told Haytham that one of my colleagues at home told his first years that 80% of what they learned during their degree would not be assessed.

I knew that if Haytham had been a student at home, I might have pushed him, in a different way, to work harder. But I did not know what motivation I could offer him that would not raise his hopes unfairly. It seemed as though he just wanted to talk.

As we walked towards the entrance to campus, Haytham told me that his father had died when he was finishing school and that he was not always able to visit his grave, because it was on the other side of the Wall. 'Sometimes a soldier will let me through,' he said.

'Once, I was walking home at 2am and some soldiers stopped me. I had my rucksack with my Playstation in it and one of them said: "What's in there? Put it on the ground." So I bent down, and he kicked me in the ass, and then they kicked me down the hill.'

# 11

# Split the air

I was sitting in the sunshine, before the final *Hamlet* class, when I felt a change in the air invading my eyes and nose. I saw people scurrying inside at every corner of the square, and I followed some other lecturers into Bard. There were students dotted throughout the building, in pairs and small groups, some of whose eyes were streaming. Some kids—either from the university or a local school, depending on who I asked—had thrown stones at Israeli soldiers, who had responded with tear gas. Only six students came to the class. Hamdi turned up briefly, but then he ran off, saying breathlessly: 'We have to defend our country.' I stopped the discussion after 45 minutes and went back to the English Department, where I ran into Tariq. He told me that the tear gas canisters had landed at the feet of a group of students, who had passed out.

For a while, it seemed as though almost every class was disrupted. In one Special Topics seminar, Tariq stood up and left the room, followed by two other men, in response to some sort of signal from the corridor. I opened the door, to find Tariq standing outside, smoking and red-eyed. He apologised and explained that the father of a friend of his had died. He had to leave to pay his respects before the funeral, which would follow very quickly.

Another class was cancelled because of a union meeting. We had not been paid again, and there were rumours that there would be another strike. I had told the students they should either turn up anyway and hand in their assignment or e-mail it to me. One woman, Dalia, said that she lived in Ramallah and I agreed to collect her essay from her uncle's jewellery shop, which was opposite the ice-cream store on Rukab, one of the main streets. When I got there, he waved to me from the window. I sat in a corner of the shop, next to a small work station, with a pan on a hob and a soldering iron. He made me a coffee and his teenage daughter told me about her school. She said that she was hoping to study sciences, which I had been told was what the brightest students were encouraged to do. (At Bard, I had been assigned a teaching assistant who was studying medicine but who read *Hamlet* with more hunger than the rest of the class.)

When I had first given the students this assignment, their response had been grumpy and reluctant. I had given them a list of ten questions, and asked them either to write an essay in response to one question or a series of five short responses. 'We do not like this sort of assignment,' one woman said. The questions were deliberately tied to the discussions we'd had about reading. For example, I asked the students to write about a character with whom they felt empathy, a story they did not finish, how the place where they read a story affected it, or about how they would re-write one of the stories. One student said, in a tone of bewilderment, 'But this means we have to have read all the stories?' and I replied 'Yes!' to general laughter.

This turned out to be the assignment where there were the biggest problems with plagiarism. I found that three of the students had plagiarised one answer from the internet, and one student had copied everything; each of her answers read like a generic summary of the story, and it quickly showed up when I searched online. The three students who had copied one answer denied it at first, then they admitted it in part, and finally they tried to get a second chance ('Please, doctor, please—give me *one* more chance'). Two of the students cried, and there was something childlike in their bargaining. I reassured them that they had still passed the assignment, but I asked them to think about whether it showed respect for me to hand in an assignment in that form—and then to deny doing it. The students were baffled by my response, since it seemed to be a criticism of them for a lack of courtesy, which they hotly denied.

I knew the likelihood was that I had missed other instances of plagiarism during the semester. I wondered often if I was being strict enough with the students, and if my policy of trying to encourage some responsibility in them actually had the opposite effect. It wasn't the only time I questioned myself. I found that I would quickly become paranoid if attendance was poor at seminars. I would search my notes to think about what we had discussed in the previous seminar, or what they had been reading, to see if there might be a problem I had not anticipated. When Haytham stopped attending for two weeks, I was convinced I had offended him. I was constantly expecting to be caught short by my lack of local knowledge, or to discover that I had made an assumption that would turn out to be erroneous, or even offensive.

I was surprised to find that the assignment where everything was plagiarised was by Lika', who was one of the sharpest students in the class, and who could sometimes be quite severe on her fellow students (and me). She was absent when I was returning the assignments, so I e-mailed her about it, and she came to see me, close to tears but putting on a brave face. She quickly conceded her mistake. I asked her why she had done it. Lika' explained that her brother had been arrested in the week the assignment was due in, and that her mother had been ill. She was distressed, because she knew that she would fail the course if she got no marks for this assignment and then she would not be able to graduate.

I felt out of my depth. I went to see Mohammed, the head of department, and asked him what I could do. He said that the Red Cross issued certificates when someone was arrested, so I could ask Lika' for proof. I asked whether Lika' could re-submit the work and he was equivocal. I suggested I could let her do it again, but tell her that the new assignment would have a maximum mark of 30 out of 40, as an acknowledgement of the original error.

He gave me permission to do this, and I told Lika'. She was reluctant ('I want my real mark!') but eventually relented.

Another issue was how to monitor student attendance. I had given up taking a register early on, because of the difficulties I initially had pronouncing students' names, and because it took so long with such a large class. But I had thus been relying on students signing their own name, which had its own risks. I decided to address this at one seminar where there was a good turnout.

We were reading the scene with Cinna the Poet. It is a peculiar interlude, designed to release some of the tensions after long speeches from Antony and Brutus have stirred up the crowds. It is often played for laughs, although it has taken a sinister turn, including in the 1930s production by Orson Welles, in which it was used to highlight the behaviour of a mob. Cinna leaves his home, while the streets are still frenzied, and is asked a series of questions by the people he meets:

1 Plebian:   What is your name?
2 Plebian:   Where are you going?
3 Plebian:   Where do you dwell?
4 Plebian:   Are you a married man or a bachelor?

The crowd confuses Cinna the Poet with his namesake, who was one of the conspirators; and yet, when the confusion has been revealed, they decide to kill him anyway: 'Kill him for his bad verses!' Noor thought that Shakespeare shared Cassius's view of the masses. They both treat them dismissively, she said, and think crowds behave brutally. She also said she was sure that the plebian who asks Cinna if he is married 'must be a woman.' Qais disagreed. 'No, this could be anyone. Like in the West Bank, you always ask someone if he is married or not, who his family is, this is just the same.' Shakespeare may be teasing himself and his audience, I pointed out, by showing the crowd turn on a poet.

The class had been full of humour, and I found myself surfing this wave of good feeling to address attendance. At the end I said that, if students were going to get a friend to sign their name on the register, they should make sure that the friend knew how to spell their name — and that only one friend signed ('It really gives the game away if your name appears three times'). There was a short silence, as if they were not sure how to respond, and then everybody laughed.

It didn't help that I was still struggling to learn a small number of the students' names. In Special Topics, when we came to discuss the Maxim Gorky story, 'Twenty-six Men and a Girl', two of the women were exceptionally sharp in the discussion, and I was ashamed that I still did not know what to call them. The story, written in 1899, is about a group of labourers making pretzels in a cellar, whose lives are occasionally enlivened by the visits of a young woman. These brief interruptions of bliss are cut short when a soldier joins the bakers. He seduces the girl, and the men turn on her.

> We worked mechanically away with our fingers and hands for hours on end, and we had grown so used to our work that we no longer even watched what we were doing. We knew each other's faces so well that every wrinkle was familiar. There was nothing to talk about and we had become accustomed to the silence [...] But silence is painful and terrifying only for those who have already said everything and who have nothing left to say; but to those who have not yet begun to talk, silence comes easily and simply.

One of the peculiar features of the story is that the narrator uses the pronoun 'we,' as if speaking on behalf of all of the bakers. We speculated about what this means: that the work the bakers do is mechanical; that they do not have a life of their own; that none of them is an 'I'; that they are 'incarcerated.' I pushed the students on why it says 'to those who have not yet begun to talk, silence comes easily and simply.' They explained why they thought the men did not speak. I kept pushing on why it says 'not begun to talk.'

'When do humans normally begin to talk?' I asked. 'Why is this celebrated as an event?'

'It is part of becoming human,' Lika' said.

\* \* \*

I was continuing to explore the West Bank with friends I was making in Ramallah. One Saturday, a group of us went to Nabi Saleh, for a play called 'Our Sign is the Stone', performed by the Freedom Bus Theatre. When we set off from Ramallah, there were rumours of clashes with settlers near Nabi Saleh, but we went anyway and there was no sign of trouble. The performance was followed by a 'playback' session, in which the actors invited members of the audience to come and tell their story, which would then be acted out. A little girl of about seven came forward. She explained that she had encountered two soldiers in her village and told them to leave. 'I said that I didn't want them there because they had killed my uncle and my friend.'

From a hilltop in Nabi Saleh, you could see a small settlement just across the valley, identifiable by its smart white houses and red roofs. (When I left the West Bank, it took me some time to adjust to the fact that small groups of houses with red roofs were not always settlements.) In the distance, we could also see construction under way on Rawabi, a 'planned Palestinian city' for which I had seen advertisements in Ramallah. During the journey home, Simon told me that he had been to visit Rawabi earlier that week, with some journalists. They were given the tour for those potentially interested in buying a property. About eight thousand (of forty thousand) had been sold thus far. The tour finished in a room where there were representatives of various banks, who were ready to sell mortgages. The city was aimed at upwardly mobile Palestinians, especially the American-born or aspiring elite.

There had been some anger among Israeli settlers about Rawabi, and protests that all contractors had to sign up to say they would not use products from the settlements. But the parallels with the settlements were eerie, not only in the architecture. There were rumours that the residents of three villages were evicted, to make way for the development, and their homes demolished; there were also suggestions that Rawabi was designed to suck in residents from Area C, which was under Israeli control, opening the way for it to be annexed. I did not know which of these rumours to believe. It is one function of living in the West Bank that one starts to see no clear distinction between conspiracy theories and likely explanations.

One weekend, I went with Simon and some other friends to Al-Walaja, a town near Bethlehem that is closed in by settlements on three sides, and which will ultimately be surrounded entirely by the Wall. For now, the work is incomplete. We drove to a road that encircles the town and we could see the edge of the Wall, and we each stood with a foot on either side of it. We also found a yellow metal door in the Wall, at the top of a hill. We prised it open and could see the sky on the other side. It was like the end of *The Truman Show*, when Truman escapes from the enclosed television studio he was made to believe was the world: a sudden encounter with the edge of reality.

When we left, we came across a gate, blocking the road Simon had planned to take. I looked it up that evening on the Activestills.org website that evening, where there was this explanation:

> A military gate [was] placed in front of Omar Hajajlah's home on the road leading from Al Walaja village to [the monastery and vineyard at] Cremisan [...] Omar's home will be left on

the 'other side' of the Separation Wall [when it is completed] and will be connected to the village through a tunnel. The family will be completely surrounded by a fence.

We diverted onto a road just above the gate, which was empty and silent. Huge mounds of barbed wire bordered it, and in places the road seemed unfinished: there were little mounds of plastic tubing sticking up out of concrete. There were signs, giving the speed limit and a warning of a sharp bend, but ultimately the road came to an abrupt stop, petering out into a track and then into farmland. We speculated that it must have been used to start building the Wall, and might be a military run-off road. We turned back and bounced down a track to a nearby checkpoint.

On the way home, Simon stopped the car at the entrance to Beit El, the Israeli settlement nearest to Ramallah. He wanted to show us a sign he had seen there:

The People of Israel have returned to their rightful place, the site where God promised this Land to our forefathers. Welcome to Beit El.

At around this time, there was a graduation party for the students in the English Department, held in a plush building in a nearby town. I had not realised the event was taking place, so I sheepishly stood in line with the other well-dressed members of staff, wearing a Batman t-shirt. The students were presented with certificates, even though they had not taken their final exams. I pulled Lynn aside, and she laughed. 'The first time I came, I looked along the line and thought: *that* one failed, and *that* one failed....' The party seemed to be a student tradition, and it was always held a couple of months before the graduation ceremony itself.

Wafa gave a short speech in English. She said at the start that

most of the friends and family in the audience would not understand it. Then the students put on a play called 'Student
Suffering', in which one of them acted out an ordinary day at Al-
Quds. It began with him being stopped and searched by an
Israeli soldier and ended with an altercation with the head of
department—effectively mimicked, with his trousers pulled up
high above his waistline—who told the student he had failed.

As I was leaving with a group of other staff, I saw Qais and
Haytham skulking at the back of the room. They were older than
many of the students who had been on stage, but they both had
a small number of modules still to complete. Qais had been at the
university, on and off, for seven years and Haytham for five
years. There were various reasons why it had taken them so long.
I wondered if, for all their complaints about the place, it might be
attractive to stay at university, where young men and women
were allowed to mix quite easily. They could thus postpone entry
into an adult world that might quickly impose the demands of
family life and in which there was a limited range of jobs.

Although I had started to feel as though I knew them well, my
knowledge of the students was all from the classroom. I had
trouble picturing how their lives would actually be beyond it.
Many of the English students would become teachers. Abd
already had a job at Rawabi. A couple of students worked part-
time in call centres, and others worked in a family business, such
as a shop or hotel.

Another strike was called towards the end of April, as we
were not paid again in March. I feared it was possible the
semester would be abandoned, or that it would resume after I
had to leave. I was told that such persistent financial problems
were unusual at the university. Yet I could also see that the
students were familiar with this kind of disruption. They were
used to the occupation playing havoc with their lives, one way or
another.

When we finally got back to class, I gave the students another of the Walid Khazendar poems that Tom Paulin had translated. I had found 'The Thin Hem' more difficult to understand. It ends:

—if he arrives
he'll split the air
like the flame on a welder's torch
but he doesn't he can't
—now all I want
is to find a fire and pour oil
right back on its flames

The poem is about a woman praying for the return of a man, a 'loved one who isn't here.'

I was walking back from the café over the road from campus one lunchtime, when I saw Lika'. She had looked upset in Special Topics and I asked her what was wrong. She said that she had been told she might fail her minor discipline and thus have to come back next year. She gave me a copy of the certificate about her brother's arrest, and then asked if I would like to see a picture of him. We walked into the entrance of the building. Hanging from the ceiling was a poster, bearing photos of five men of varying ages, all from the local area. Lika' told me they were all from a political movement, a small one which I had not heard of before. Her brother was 22, a year older than her, and they looked alike, each with a thin nose, so their eyes sat close together with a peculiar intensity. She said he was in Ofer prison and that they had not been allowed to see him. The date of his trial had been delayed several times.

The certificate she gave me read:

TO WHOM IT MAY CONCERN
This attestation is valid only if the English and Arabic parts match each other.

According to the information received from the Israeli Authorities, the International Committee of the Red Cross attests that:

Mr [........]

From NABLUS [ID no.]

Was arrested by the Israeli authorities on 18.04.2013

He is to date: Awaiting trial

Length of sentence/administrative period:

XXXXXXXXXXXXXXXXXXXXX

He/She was released on: XXXXXXXXXXXXXXXXXXXXXXXX

# 12

# My country's friend

The soldier asked me where I was from.

'London,' I said, showing him my passport.

The man standing next to him, who was a settler, interjected: 'Are you a football fan?' He was plump and was wearing a slim-fitting white shirt. He had been talking loudly to the soldiers and gesticulating, as we approached.

'Fulham,' I said, feeling myself take shallow gulps of air.

The settler laughed and told me that his friends in London all supported Spurs.

One of the soldiers had turned to Khalid, who had produced his wallet.

'You know what, I'm really sorry, but all I have on me is my university card,' he said.

He showed them a small Leeds University library card with his picture on it.

'Are you a Leeds United fan?' asked the settler.

Khalid nodded.

When we had left the Ibrahimi Mosque, we had made a decision without speaking. I gave Khalid my camera, which he hung around his neck, so that he looked like a tourist. At the bottom of the street below the mosque, there were two soldiers standing behind a small temporary fence. We walked alongside the fence and up to the corner, where this road met Shuhada Street, which is where the soldiers stopped us.

Hebron, which is known as Al-Khalil in Arabic, is a large city, which stretches out into villages and farmland. From the *servees*, Khalid pointed out the village his family is from. Later, we passed farmland to the right of the road and, to the left, a refugee camp, encased in wire. This section of farmland seemed scarred, empty other than the stumps of trees on the perimeter, which had been cut down to ensure the security of an Israeli settlement beyond them.

The city is predominantly Palestinian, but there is a small Israeli settlement in the centre, so it is divided into different areas of control. The most contentious point in the city is the mosque, which adjoins a synagogue, and which in the Jewish faith is known as the Cave of the Patriarchs.

We had got to the mosque through narrow streets that were mostly deserted. We passed a clothes stall, where untidy piles of children's wear were stacked on a wall and hung on coat hangers behind it, flat against a wire fence. Behind the fence was a clump of barbed wire, which stood in front of a concrete wall. Just peeking out above it was a balcony and the upper windows of a building, which were part of an Israeli street. Further on, there was a wire fence covering the street above us. The market lies directly beneath Israeli settlements and the wire above was littered with empty bottles, plastic packages, coat hangers and sweet wrappers thrown by the settlers towards the Palestinian street below. The stalls were a mixture of clothes for locals and trinkets for tourists. But the stall-keepers' attempts to attract my attention were half-hearted. Khalid explained that many of the shopkeepers opened up as a gesture of defiance, not in the expectation that they could make much money.

On the other side of the mosque is Shuhada Street, once the central marketplace in town, which has been closed to Palestinians since a massacre at the mosque in 1994. Khalid told me that he remembered visiting the street when he was a child. 'Hebron is the first place I heard gunfire. There were all these people running towards us. I asked my Dad if we were going to be killed.'

After the soldiers had let us through, Khalid kept hold of my camera as we made our way down Shuhada Street, so the pictures I have from our walk are his. The first two were taken when we had walked about a hundred yards and then turned back to look at the street. There were about a dozen one-storey shops on either side, their beige metal shutters closed. Almost the only relic of activity was a ladder, which stood about halfway down on the right, its feet resting against the pavement and its top leaning against the roof. The wide expanse of the road was empty. For the second picture, Khalid zoomed in on the very end of the street, where it curves off to the right. The soldiers had disappeared from view, but Khalid had glimpsed the young settler we had encountered, still standing on the edge of the pavement, his skullcap visible at the back of his head and his white shirt spilling untidily over his trousers.

The next picture showed a sign for tourists, which read: 'These stores were closed by the IDF for security reasons after Arabs began the "Oslo War" (aka The Second Intifada) in September 2000, attacking, wounding and murdering Jews on this road.' Another sign read: 'These buildings were constructed on land purchased by the Hebron Jewish community in 1807. This land was stolen by Arabs following the murder of 67 Hebron Jews in 1929. We demand justice! Return our property to us!'

The streets were mostly deserted, but we passed a clutch of soldiers, and then a small group of children. There was an older girl holding hands with a younger one, and several boys throwing water balloons. One of the photographs shows a boy of about twelve gliding down the slight hill on his skateboard. The next one is of another row of closed shops, each with a green metal hood. There was faded Arabic writing on the first shop and Khalid explained that it had been a pet shop. Two Israeli flags hung from a lamppost outside.

The end of Shuhada Street is blocked by a beige portakabin, and we were stopped by a group of soldiers just before it. One of them inspected my passport, and Khalid again rehearsed his story about being a student. The soldier nearest to us indicated that we could go. 'Take care of this place for us,' Khalid said, as we turned. I knew he was pushing his luck, and the solider seemed to hesitate. I touched Khalid on the elbow and we walked quickly away.

\* \* \*

I said to the students: 'Imagine that instead of Caesar being a political leader, he is your teacher; imagine that I am Caesar. Some students love me, and others hate me. What will happen after the ones who hate me have got rid of me?'

'Civil war,' said Amjad quietly.

'Some people will run away.'

'There will be a lot of corruption and arguments.'

We read Act IV scene iii, which is an argument between the conspirators Brutus and Cassius, in which they sound almost like lovers. I read Brutus's part and Abd read Cassius. The argument starts because Brutus has condemned a man called Lucius Pella for taking bribes, after Cassius supported him. Brutus accuses Cassius of being greedy (perhaps even of taking bribes himself) and Cassius says that, if anyone other than Brutus had said that, he would have killed him. The students laughed a little at the pantomime elements: 'I denied you not,' 'You did,' 'I did not.'

After class, I put a quotation on Facebook from an essay about the play by William Hazlitt from his 1817 book *Characters of Shakespear's Plays*:

> The whole design of the conspirators to liberate their country fails from the generous temper and over-weening confidence of Brutus in the goodness of their cause and the assistance of others... Those who mean well themselves think well of others... That humanity and honesty which dispose men to resist injustice and tyranny render them unfit to cope with the cunning and power of those who are opposed to them... Cassius was better cut out for a conspirator.

A discussion followed, to which Qais contributed:

> Haha, this is a surprisingly identical interpretation of the way
> I thought of the main characters today... I was thinking of
> comparing this to the Arab countries. Putting devilish ideology
> aside, Brutus and Cassius are no different from those who
> overthrew [the] kings of Iraq and Syria over decades ago in
> hope of "change"... Finding so many similarities, I am amazed
> how they never thought they'd end up just like the conspir-
> ators from *Julius Caesar*! Also, conspirators always have so
> much confidence in a way that they believe they should be the
> ones to lead the masses... Brutus thought the people were too
> immature to resort to, in the same way Al Bitar and Michel
> Aflaq thought the people of Syria at the time needed to be
> educated (Ba'athingly) the way he saw best, then liberated.

We were pushed for time by the point we reached Act V, in which
the conspiracy unravels. We paused over a confusing moment on
the battlefield in which Antony's soldiers come across a man
named Lucilius, who claims:

> ... I am Brutus, Marcus Brutus, I,
> Brutus, my country's friend. Know me for Brutus!

I let the students' confusion settle for a moment, and then asked
them why Lucilius would pretend to the soldiers that he is
someone else. 'He wants to protect Brutus,' one woman said. 'No,
he is protecting himself, because they will kill Lucilius, but they
might capture Brutus, but keep him alive.'

Brutus and Antony suddenly seem almost like colleagues at
the end, after being enemies throughout: they have shared
experience, as survivors. In contrast, Caesar's nephew Octavius,
who inherits power, sounds high-pitched and out of tune as he
closes the play: 'So call the field to rest, and let's away / To part

the glories of this happy day.' Anwar suggested (acutely) that, when Octavius talks about honouring Brutus in his death, he sounds like a politician, as though he is doing this because he knows it might be popular. The students also noted the loose threads at the end. For example, Antony spares Lucilius, which they pointed out was similar to the conspirators sparing Antony.

\* \* \*

I asked the students in Special Topics to tell me about *'adab,'* the Arabic word for literature. They explained that the word had a relationship to 'politeness,' but also to 'the arts' in general—for example, it was used to describe 'The Arts Building' on campus. I asked if anyone could think of a word that was similar to the word 'literature' in English. It was the worst kind of question you can ask as a teacher. I was fishing for a particular answer, hoping someone would say 'literate.'

I could see Haytham feeling the weight of a contribution he might make before he spoke. He smiled. 'Furniture,' he said crisply. We all laughed, and I was about to move on. 'Hang on,' I said. 'I'll take that. What is "furniture?"'

There was a baffled silence. I asked the students to name items of furniture—a chair, a table, a desk and so on. 'But can we come up for a rule for furniture? It is always something you sit on? Is it always something you have in your home?' We played around with different definitions, edging closer to something conclusive, but each time finding an exception that did not fit the rule.

I asked the students how they would spot the difference if I gave them two stories and told them only one of the two was 'literature.' We talked about the differences in language there might be between the two stories, and that one might recognise a type or genre of literature in one story. But again, we could not come up with a simple rule. Haytham asked whether the Bible was considered literature, which led to a good discussion about whether literature needed to be true or fictional, and whether we always know the difference.

'So, who decides which literature is studied on your degree?' My question was met with blank looks.

'You do,' said one woman.

'On what basis?' I asked.

A man gave an answer I did not hear properly, and I asked him to repeat it.

'Your knowledge,' he said, more loudly.

'Ah,' I said. 'I thought you said "your mother...."'

We all laughed. I knew it was a moment that would have been impossible earlier in the term.

Haytham had been pushing a slightly different argument in the discussion about the Bible. He wanted to know whether there were limits to what literature could include. He pointed out that in Palestine you would know one of the stories was not literature if it included descriptions of 'physical love.' He was worried that literature was used too often in Palestine to enforce a particular moral perspective. This led us on to a discussion about whether literature is moral and polite or whether it can be subversive. I pointed out that Haytham's comment about 'furniture' had been subversive in a good way, that it had turned the discussion upside down.

In both courses, I was starting to prepare students for their final exam. In Special Topics, I was going to ask the students to debate a statement from two points of view. We held a practice debate on the statement: 'Literature is a more effective art form than film.' At the beginning, I asked the class to vote on whether they agreed, disagreed or didn't know. A slim majority disagreed and most of the students did not vote, in spite of my prompting. Haytham suggested that we needed a category for those who 'don't know if they don't know.' This led nicely into the idea of abstentions, although I knew that Haytham had meant those who were not thinking. Ruba said that it was hard to judge what one thought because the statement was vague.

The debate was structured so that one argument was made proposing the motion, then two opposing, followed by two proposing, two more for each side and then a final point from the opposition. The comparison with film brought out real feeling, including among those who felt reading was boring. The first proposal was along the lines that literature has been around for longer and existed all over the world, and that it influenced film, for example in the Harry Potter series. Wafa lead the charge; she was the most committed reader in the class. Others said that film was better because everything was imagined in it, and because it could take us closer to literature of some kinds: we understand Shakespeare better when his work is performed. There was also a nice argument that even if literature was more effective, this includes *bad* effects, so it did not mean literature had won.

'What about *Titanic*?' asked Haytham. 'This is a film that everybody has seen and it makes people cry. Literature does not do that.'

'Did you cry, Haytham?' I asked.

He smiled.

This led to a discussion about whether film was more effective *because* it reached more people.

At the end, I asked the students to vote again. A substantial majority, 14 to 7, were now against the motion. But one woman said she was confused because she agreed with different arguments from each side. I called this don't know 'plus.' It was perfect. In the exam, I said, the students would need to come to some sort of complex conclusion rather than a vote; they would need to weigh how much their own conclusion fell on either side.

One evening, Haytham posted a message on Facebook:

When they ask you why do you wanna leave this country, answer with the following;- This is a country that whenever you decide to be your self it shuts you down. This is a country that's filled with people claiming to be Muslims but they're far away from Islam. This is a country with a society that's controlled by a fictional fame that never existed and will never benefit them a damn. This is a country that whenever you want to go around you have to jump like a clown. This is a country that only reminds me of something Brown! Still looking for an answer?

The post prompted a fierce debate. Basilah lamented that Haytham's comments were 'full of misery and self hate.' She added: 'We don't have a country yet to rail against; perhaps we should wait until we do before we curse it.' When someone challenged her, she clarified her position: 'In our situation as Palestinians, we have to be careful about how we [criticize our country]. Criticizing is one thing; being down on ourselves is another. So many young people feel discouraged and actually end up leaving.' Haytham replied:

> Well, just because I criticized the country it doesn't necessarily mean that I hate it or I hate being in it [...] I'm only criticizing and hoping that the parts that I have criticized [will] get better and better and that pretty much will show my love to this country by pointing out the bad habits that should be rearranged in order for this country to develop its way of growing up. So I'm pretty proud of being a Palestinian but I am disappointed of seeing my beloved country collapsing.

I e-mailed Haytham, to say that his remarks reminded me of something Stanley Cavell had once written: 'Those who voice politically radical wishes for this country may forget the radical hopes it holds for itself.' Cavell's point was partly that criticising one's own country could also be a version of patriotism.

Haytham insisted on coming to see me in the office, to teach me about what would happen when I left. He told me that I should deny that I had been in the West Bank or that I knew any Palestinians, and that the Israeli security forces at Ben Gurion airport in Tel Aviv might check my Facebook account or my e-mail. I was already feeling paranoid, as my Facebook account had been hacked a few days before. Haytham also warned me that there were spies at the university and that the Israelis would already know everything I had been doing.

'They must be the only country in the world who don't need any more spies. If someone comes and volunteers they say: "No, thanks—we're full up...."'

Haytham described being in Ma'ale Adummim once and talking to a soldier, who offered him chocolate, a cigarette—and who was trying to tempt him, in a friendly way, to become an informer. He feigned incompetence, saying he was lazy and only interested in girls. 'And then I come back here and everyone's like: "Hey, Haytham, why do you have a beard? Are you joining Hamas now?"'

We wandered out into the hallway, so that Haytham could have a cigarette. 'I could get out,' he said. 'If it wasn't for this green tree in my pocket.' He told me that his uncle was an 'Israeli Arab' and had suggested that Haytham marry his daughter, so that he could have a blue ID card instead.

'Were you tempted?'

'No, it's just gonna mean more problems.'

I asked him about a job as a teaching assistant that I knew staff in the department wanted him to apply for when he graduated. Ahmed had told me that if Haytham took the job they would try to get funding for him to go abroad and do an MA.

'Yeah, but then I'd have to come back.'

I told Haytham that I had been thinking about staying.

'If you were born here, you wouldn't want to. I would never have children here, so they would have to live like this.'

He described how close his family's house was to the Wall and told me that sometimes he put his music on loud, just because he knew that the soldiers could hear it.

'You're here because you pity us, aren't you?'

# 13

# Schools to me

I had put off meeting Eliana until I was nearly due to leave the West Bank. I could never get used to crossing from east to west Jerusalem. Israel took over Jerusalem in the war in 1967, and you could still buy postcards in Ramallah that stated that the city was part of Jordan. It has been divided into two halves, which co-exist in uneasy proximity. East Jerusalem is considered occupied territory under international law, although it is now on the Israeli side of the Wall. There is no physical barrier, yet it felt jarring to walk from the packed market around the Damascus Gate to the broad streets and European-style shops and cafés just half a mile away. Eliana and I had a mutual friend in London, and she had been suggesting that we meet up since I arrived. In late May, I made the trip to have dinner with her.

Eliana's hand shook with nerves as we greeted one another. While we were still looking politely at the menu, she asked: 'What is Ramallah like? We cannot go there.'

Eliana was a teacher, and she told me that she was a couple of years away from retirement. She described the growing bureau-cratic load in her school, and I told her a little about the teaching I had done at Al-Quds.

Towards the end of the meal, as we were waiting for the bill, we talked in a stop-start way about the political situation, mostly in pleasantries. I thought the conversation had finished, when Eliana returned to it, as if she was impulsively touching a sore spot.

'The real problem,' she said, 'is that Palestinian children are taught to hate us.'

'The funny thing,' I said, 'is that they would say the same thing about Israelis.'

I knew, as I said it, that I had hit the wrong note, that I was responding too much in kind.

'It isn't funny,' she replied.

I asked Eliana where she lived and she named a suburb in the north of Jerusalem. 'It was one of the first to be developed after the 1967 war. My father bought the land and cultivated it from *nothing*. But now there are problems. The whole area has become totally dominated by the Orthodox—and they... Well, it's all very different now. So, I will probably move. I am being driven from my home. And we're all Jews!'

The next day, I had been invited to meet with senior staff at Al-Quds to discuss my impressions of the university. I sat at one corner of a long table, opposite four administrators, three men and one woman, all of whom were smoking. The questions they asked me were the same ones that senior academics had posed to me on other occasions. 'Tell us about the problems you have encountered'; 'How is the standard of our students, compared to those you teach at home?'; 'What could we do to improve things?' It felt as though they were anticipating criticism from me; taking sides with a Western academic against their own students. I became banal and upbeat in response: 'My students have been wonderful, I've learnt a great deal from them....'

There is another answer I might have given, to them and to Eliana, which I could not articulate at the time. Not long after I graduated, in 2002, I applied for a job at Liverpool Hope University. A few weeks later, I arrived home and my friend, James, was leaning out of the kitchen window of our first-floor flat. We had both been unemployed for the summer after graduation, and one morning we'd had a row after he had finished the last of the bread; eventually our anger dissolved into laughter. He shouted down to me from the window: 'I think you've got a job!'

It wasn't the job I had applied for, but I had been asked to teach on an Access course. The tutor had quit just before the second year of the course, and they needed someone to teach *Othello*. The class met on Wednesdays from 6pm at Colwell Primary School in Dovecot. It was a long, cavernous building that was otherwise deserted at night. On the first evening, I drove the circuitous route I had been given to the school and parked up outside. It was in the middle of a housing estate, the central road of which was blocked off to prevent teenagers from racing their cars along it. Our classroom was at the centre of the building, and would be the only one lit.

In the reception area, I found a few of the students hanging around, chatting with the caretaker. 'Are you new?' a woman called Jackie asked me. I nodded sheepishly. 'Don't worry,' she said, patting my elbow: 'You'll soon settle in.'

My abiding memory of that first evening is of standing on a chair, trying to explain that the stage at the Globe Theatre was divided between an upper and lower section. As I boomed out a bit of the first scene of the play, I looked down and saw a dozen sceptical faces looking back at me. Later, one of the students said: 'I thought maybe you were going to kill us.'

In the second week, I asked the students how they were getting on with a research project they had been working on over the summer. They had each been asked to select a novel and to write an essay about it. Most of the students raised problems about structure or about finishing their assignment. But one woman, called Julie, replied: 'I haven't started it.' Julie was in her 30s. As she spoke, her whole body was radiating defiance.

'Why not? You've had a whole summer to work on it.'

I was surprised to find I had clicked into the role of the teacher.

'The novel I chose is really boring. I don't have anything to say about it.'

The essay was due to be submitted in two weeks, so it was too late for Julie to choose another book. I suggested that we should have a chat about it, while the other students did some work on their project. Julie had chosen *Brighton Rock* by Graham Greene, which I hadn't read. I asked her to tell me about one thing she liked in the novel, even if it was only a sentence or a character. Julie talked for about five minutes about Ida and Rose, the two main female characters, explaining their struggles and how they were described. Eventually, I interrupted her: 'So why aren't you writing about that?'

'Because that isn't what my question's about.'

'But this should be about what interests you.'

'I'm not being funny, but I've just spent a year being told not to write "I think". Now are you telling me this should be personal?'

Julie later told me that she had worked as a dinner lady at one of the private schools in the city, and that she had signed up for the Access course because she got fed up with watching the students go off to university.

A couple of weeks later, Julie came up to me before class and said she'd been trying to read *Othello*, but that she had a few questions about it. She thought if I could just answer them, she would be able to get to grips with the play. She handed me a small scrap of paper. One of the questions was: 'I don't understand why Iago is doing this to Othello. Has Othello done something to him, or has he just got it in for him?'

In another class, in the spring of 2003, I gave the students some extracts from accounts of life in Israel and the occupied territories, including Jeff Halper's description of attending a protest against the demolition of Palestinian homes:

In the end an army jeep came and I was tossed in the back. We drove up the security road to Pisgat Ze'ev, where I was told to go home. Walking over to a bus stop, dirty, smelly from the sewage, my clothes torn, a woman asks me what happened. Reluctantly I tell her that I was trying to resist the demolition of some of the homes of her neighbours in Shuafat, nodding in the direction of the camp. The reaction was painfully predictable. "Terrorists! They're trying to move their houses into our neighbourhood! Why don't they build with permits, like we do? They don't pay their taxes and expect free houses and services! This is our country. When I came here from Morocco...." The bus pulls up, we get on and she tells the driver: "Leave him off in Shuafat. They'll kill him there."

We had a good discussion about the extracts. At the end of the class, I saw that one woman, Tina, was still sitting down, as others packed up their bags and left. As I was collecting my books and handouts, ready to leave, I caught her eye.

'It's funny,' she said. 'I've heard about this on the news all the time. But I always thought it was a civil war.'

E.P. Thompson, in a 1968 lecture called 'Education and Experience', concluded that:

There is no automatic correlation between 'real feeling and just sense' and educational attainments. But the pressures of our time are leading us to confuse the two—and university teachers, who are not always noted for their humility, are often ready to assent to the confusion. To strike the balance between intellectual rigour and respect for experience is always difficult. But the balance today is seriously awry.

Thompson was trying to define (and defend) extra-mural work in UK universities, which since he wrote has been all but extinguished. The old extra-mural departments offered courses outside of normal hours for students who could not otherwise access higher education. I have spent the ten years of my career so far working in the dying embers of this tradition. The phrase 'real feeling and just sense' is from *The Prelude*, where in Book 13, Wordsworth writes of walks he had taken in a rural community:

When I began to inquire,
To watch and question those I met, and held
Familiar talk with them, the lonely roads
Were schools to me in which I daily read
With most delight the passions of mankind,
There saw into the depths of human souls,
Souls that appear to have no depth at all
To vulgar eyes. And now convinced at heart
How little that to which alone we give
The name of education hath to do
With real feeling and just sense...

There are times when education provides a vital structure and enables us to transcend our own perspective, or prejudice; to realise, as Tina so honestly articulated, that we make assumptions all of the time that are false, without even knowing they are assumptions. Or that those assumptions are made for us. Yet, as Thompson saw, educational institutions contrive their own distinctive forms of prejudice too; they have their own blind spots.

I sometimes had doubts about how useful I could be to the students at Al-Quds, and I felt sure that an expert in Palestinian (or postcolonial, or comparative) literature would have more to offer. I doubted my subject too, wishing I had more practical skills to offer. Yet I had also moments of naïve delight. 'I never knew ancient literature was this cool,' Qais wrote to me. I knew what he meant: 'Shakespeare is *amazing*,' I found myself thinking. And it was Shakespeare's plays, above all, that offered my students a space to reflect on their lives, without seeming to do so. It was partly the distance from them, the invisible borders they had to cross out of their own experience, that gave them a space to engage with the plays imaginatively. Shakespeare himself, of course, is giving nothing away. He survived in his own times by rarely revealing his own point of view. Many of his contemporaries were gaoled for the words they had actors speak on stage. When the classes worked, it was because of a sort of alchemy between what we read and the students' experiences. And, of course, the pleasure split both ways for me, since I got to cross borders both into Shakespeare and into my students' experiences; each was a 'school to me.'

It would be easy to patronise the students at Al-Quds, and I heard colleagues (both Palestinian and American) do this, for their lack of sophistication or for their reluctance to read. It would be easy too to mistake inarticulacy for lack of feeling. But my students at Al-Quds showed extraordinary creativity, courage and humour in their daily lives, and in navigating the obstacles they faced, even in getting to class. Formal educational environments are sometimes very bad at allowing students to utilise the 'real feeling and just sense' they have brought with them to the classroom. They can also reward particular kinds of obedience. When I have taught groups of clever and privileged undergraduates in the UK, I have sometimes found a peculiar pattern emerges. The students may be sophisticated, well-read, and articulate; they can be a joy to teach. But they are not always *thinking*, in part because they may not have had to (although this is a generalisation in its own way).

In the UK, universities ignore or exclude certain kinds of experience routinely and structurally, now even more than when E.P. Thompson spoke in 1968. We collude in a belief that educational attainment is the only measure of intelligence. We thus deprive ourselves of access to large swathes of experience, by denying entry to those whose lives have been the most demanding or by demanding conformity from them. In the years to come, this will be a challenge in international recruitment as well as domestically. Universities in the UK are under immense pressure to take increasing numbers of international students, because they pay higher fees. Inevitably, this means recruiting from elites of various kinds. We make only limited adjustments for the vast numbers of those who cannot afford to pay, including the perpetually or temporarily dispossessed. There is much that we miss out on, as a consequence. For example, these students have practical knowledge of ideas that we too often study as abstract concepts in the humanities, such as injustice and how it feels to be denied one's humanity. There is much that the students at Al-Quds, for example, could teach their counterparts in the UK.

As Thompson articulated it:

> Democracy will realize itself—if it does—in our *whole* society and our *whole* culture: and, for this to happen, the universities need the abrasion of different worlds of experience, in which ideas are brought to the test of life.

The Palestinian poet, Rafeef Ziadah, makes another version of Thompson's argument in 'We teach life, sir!':

> And I perfected my English and I learned my UN resolutions. But still, he asked me, Ms. Ziadah, don't you think that everything would be resolved if you would just stop teaching so much hatred to your children?
> Pause.
> [...]
> Rafeef, remember to smile.
> Pause.
> We teach life, sir!

A number of my students quoted this poem to me and I quickly fell in love with it. It underlines the futility of some of what Palestinians are 'taught': to speak English or to 'learn' about international law. The retort 'We teach life, sir!', which is repeated throughout the poem, is not only defiant, it is also celebratory. The poem speaks to a polite audience who may be unused to such horrors ('remember to smile. / Pause.'). Yet it transforms all that is happening to the speaker into a resolute claim for the power of what she has: 'We teach life, sir!'

\* \* \*

The students organised an end-of-term party, which happened to coincide with my last day on campus. It was in a large, light hall in a building I had not been in before. They had prepared sweets, chocolates and cakes and decorated the room with balloons. There was a disconcerting lull, at the start of the party, as if after all of this preparation nobody was sure what to do. Eventually, some formalities broke out. The students presented several of the staff with certificates and I managed to say my thank-yous and goodbyes in Arabic, with a couple of corrections from the audience.

In our last class, I had asked the students to write a story about the semester. Tariq had written one in which it turned out I was James Bond. There was a series of improbable events, and then he quoted himself saying: 'But, dude, this is madness! This is Al-Quds University!' Tariq told me he was relieved he would not have to travel from Hebron to Abu Dis any more. I asked if he remembered our encounter on my first visit to campus in 2011, when he had said it was all a waste of time. 'No,' he said, 'I don't remember that.' He smiled. 'But it sounds like something I would say.'

Haytham had come to see me in the office before the party and we had sat smoking in the hallway. He had failed one of his other courses and would have to repeat it the following year. It was a language module, which many students found challenging and which he had nicknamed 'rocket science.' He was worried that the lecturer whose class he had failed would be at the party. 'I'll tell him it's not you,' I said. 'We'll say you are Haytham's twin brother.' But Haytham sat in the corridor outside the hall, perched on a windowsill. When I looked out just after the speeches, a small crowd of students was standing in a circle around him.

After the party, I walked up the hill to get the *servees* with a few students, who were chatting to me in Arabic, testing out which phrases I knew. Lynn walked ahead of us with Haytham and when we got to the top of the hill they both stopped, ready to walk home. Haytham stood slightly apart, his bag slung across his shoulders, and lit another cigarette. 'Well, goodbye doctor,' he said. Lynn and I said an affectionate farewell.

I spent most of my last few days in Ramallah marking exams. In the midst of this, I got a text from Lynn: 'Protesters made a hole in Wall behind my house and there were clashes all night. House is still filled with tear gas. Lots of shooting, door to door.' The students were full of surprises again. The final question in the Shakespeare exam had asked them to choose one of Octavius, Portia or Calpurnia from *Julius Caesar* and explain how the story of the play would be different if it was told from his or her point of view. This was an extract from Noor's rewriting:

If the story was told from Calpurnia's point of view, the play would start with Caesar, describing him as a noble, humble man, who freed Rome from Pompey's tyranny, and became a good king. Then she would move to her dream, and how scared she is for her husband, and she would describe how she tried to convince him not to go to see the public. After the death of Caesar she would go through deep sorrow, and she would decide to seek revenge. She would call Antony before the conspirators do, and tell him to go and see the conspirators when they call him, and she would tell him how to manipulate them and the commoners. She also would give him the letter and tell him to pretend that this letter was Caesar's will. She wouldn't tell the audience about Brutus' and Cassius' conversations, and she would add to the play a description (a full description) of the corruption that happened in Rome after Caesar's death, and I think that the play would end with her and Mark Antony getting married.

In the Special Topics exam, some of the students had debated the topic 'We should study Palestinian literature instead of English literature at university'. One student wrote:

Yes, we should study Palestinian literature instead of English literature in the university. Because we are Plastinian [sic] not English people, so we have to know more about our literature. For example, I'm third year student in the university, and I don't know anything about Palestinian literature, I just know Shakespeare and T.S. Eliot, and that thing not god [sic] for a Palestinian person.

Lika' wrote:

As we are Palestinians, we should study our literature. Every nation must know everything about it, history, art, culture, and tradition. There must be people within a country [that] don't know anything or don't know many things about their country's literature. That's why a country must teach its literature. For me, for example, I don't know all things about Palestine literature. I once heard information about our literature, I become like, REALLY!

When I had nearly finished marking the Shakespeare exams, I checked my e-mail and found that I had a message from a student called Shadia. She'd taken the Shakespeare exam the day before. Shadia wrote: 'On 12 May, the Israeli army imprisoned my brother, at 3am they came to our house, they broke the doors window and took him, they also took my soul with him.' He was younger than her, in his late teens. The family had been allowed no contact with him after his arrest, and no reason had been given for it. She was worried that she might have failed the final exam, but she realised there was nothing I could do. This was not the first time I had received this sort of message from a student, but I feared she was right. I was not going back to campus—I had agreed to leave the exam scripts with Ahmed. I paced around my apartment, not wanting to check her grade. When I finally looked at her paper, Shadia had got 38 out of 40.

I no longer think that *Romeo and Juliet* is a love story. When I've read it in the past, the lovers have predominated. But it's a fleeting affair, and they may be mismatched as a couple; many readers have noted that Juliet outgrows Romeo. While we were reading the play in Abu Dis, the danger that the lovers are in, which had once been the background to the story, suddenly became the foreground. One line, which I had never noticed before, kept coming back to me. Juliet has just asked Romeo how he made it to her balcony. He replies:

Romeo:      With love's light wings did I o'erperch these walls,
                For stony limits cannot hold love out,
                And what love can do, that dares love attempt;
                Therefore thy kinsmen are no stop to me.
Juliet:        If they do see thee, they will murder thee.
                (II, ii, 66-70)

You could read Juliet's words, like Romeo's, as teenage hyperbole. But I now think she is in earnest.

# Acknowledgements

An earlier version of Chapter 1 appeared on *Mondoweiss*. I would like to thank the editors for permission to reprint it here. Patricia Ferguson and Jeremy Harding made many helpful suggestions about a draft of that article. I am grateful to the United Nations for permission to reproduce a map of Israel, the West Bank and Gaza.

Some of those whose influence is felt most in this book are not thanked here because they appear in the story, usually under a new name. I am especially grateful to my colleagues in the English Department at Al-Quds, for their kindness and for the trust they placed in me, and to all those who befriended me in both Abu Dis and Ramallah. I am grateful to those students who gave permission for me to include extracts from their work.

The semester I spent in the West Bank was made possible by two supportive heads of department, Mohammed Thawabteh at Al-Quds and Roger Middleton in Bristol. My original connection to the university was Sari Nusseibeh, who I introduced at the Bath Festival in 2008. I am grateful to him and to Sarah LeFanu, who asked me to chair that event. I would like to thank the curry night regulars: Marijke Peters, Merit Hietanen, Zara Mesbah, Marie-Pierre Py, Matthew Richard, Amber Savage and Joe Slowey. Mohammad Abu Hilwa taught me much about the Arabic language and about Palestine. Casey Asprooth-Jackson and Stephanie Saldana were generous colleagues at Al-Quds Bard.

My stint at Al-Quds was inspired by the examples set for me by Neil Hertz and my father, David Sperlinger, and I would not have started this book without their encouragement. Vivienne Jackson, Josie McLellan and Theo Savvas each read a draft with sensitivity and improved it beyond measure. Jess Farr-Cox saved me from a variety of errors. The students who I have re-named

Haytham, Sami and Qais also read an earlier version and made many helpful suggestions. I hope that I have learned something from Haytham's honesty.

While I have been writing this book, family and friends have offered practical support and encouragement. I would like to thank Claire Blencowe, Steve Bloomfield, Julian Brigstocke, Jo Carruthers, Ranji Devadason, Daniel Pablo Garay, Jack Goolden, Katie Goolden, Lorna Henry, Julie Hessey, Hester Jones, Jana Kirwan, Madhu Krishnan, Amy Laurent, Aleks Lewicki, Michael Malay, Lisa Oliver, Chris Penfold, Sian Penfold, Richard Pettigrew, Hannah Sheppard, Anthea Sperlinger, Mike Sperlinger, Rhiannon Taylor, Alice Walker, Dan Whillis, Jane Wright and Vanda Zajko. I am indebted to the staff at Number 12 café in Easton for their patience, when they were doing little business from the time that I spent there. I am especially grateful to two *menschen*, Sam Kirwan and Philip Shoyer.

My largest debt is to my students at Al-Quds and I hope that I have in some way repaid it in these pages. They taught me more than I can say and the book is for them.

Contemporary culture has eliminated both the concept of the public and the figure of the intellectual. Former public spaces – both physical and cultural – are now either derelict or colonized by advertising. A cretinous anti-intellectualism presides, cheerled by expensively educated hacks in the pay of multinational corporations who reassure their bored readers that there is no need to rouse themselves from their interpassive stupor. The informal censorship internalized and propagated by the cultural workers of late capitalism generates a banal conformity that the propaganda chiefs of Stalinism could only ever have dreamt of imposing. Zer0 Books knows that another kind of discourse – intellectual without being academic, popular without being populist – is not only possible: it is already flourishing, in the regions beyond the striplit malls of so-called mass media and the neurotically bureaucratic halls of the academy. Zer0 is committed to the idea of publishing as a making public of the intellectual. It is convinced that in the unthinking, blandly consensual culture in which we live, critical and engaged theoretical reflection is more important than ever before.